Cambridge Elements ≡

Elements in New Religious Movements
Series Editor
Rebecca Moore
San Diego State University
Founding Editor
†James R. Lewis
Wuhan University

ANTICULTISM IN FRANCE

Scientology, Religious Freedom, and the Future of New and Minority Religions

Donald A. Westbrook
San José State University

CAMBRIDGE
UNIVERSITY PRESS

Shaftesbury Road, Cambridge CB2 8EA, United Kingdom

One Liberty Plaza, 20th Floor, New York, NY 10006, USA

477 Williamstown Road, Port Melbourne, VIC 3207, Australia

314–321, 3rd Floor, Plot 3, Splendor Forum, Jasola District Centre,
New Delhi – 110025, India

103 Penang Road, #05–06/07, Visioncrest Commercial, Singapore 238467

Cambridge University Press is part of Cambridge University Press & Assessment,
a department of the University of Cambridge.

We share the University's mission to contribute to society through the pursuit of
education, learning and research at the highest international levels of excellence.

www.cambridge.org
Information on this title: www.cambridge.org/9781009551854

DOI: 10.1017/9781009551816

First published 2024

A catalogue record for this publication is available from the British Library.

ISBN 978-1-009-55185-4 Hardback
ISBN 978-1-009-55180-9 Paperback
ISSN 2635-232X (online)
ISSN 2635-2311 (print)

Cambridge University Press & Assessment has no responsibility for the persistence
or accuracy of URLs for external or third-party internet websites referred to in this
publication and does not guarantee that any content on such websites is, or will
remain, accurate or appropriate.

Anticultism in France

Scientology, Religious Freedom, and the Future of New and Minority Religions

Elements in New Religious Movements

DOI: 10.1017/9781009551816
First published online: May 2024

Donald A. Westbrook
San José State University

Author for correspondence: Donald A. Westbrook, donald.westbrook@sjsu.edu

Abstract: This Element introduces readers to the problem of anticultism and antireligious movements in France. The first section offers an overview of anticultism in France, including the paradoxical place of modern French secularism (*laïcité*) that has shaped a culture prejudiced against minority religions and new religions (*sectes* or "cults") and impacted Europe more broadly. This includes state-sponsored expressions, in particular MIVILUDES, an organization funded by the French government to monitor cultic or sectarian deviances. The second section takes up the case of the American-born Church of Scientology, tracing its history in the country since the late 1950s and how it has become a major focus of anticultists in France. The final section concludes with reflections on the future of new and minority religions in France. A timeline provides major dates in the history of anticultism in modern French history, with a focus on items of relevance to Scientology in France.

Keywords: France, anticultism, new religious movements, Scientology, minority religions

ISBNs: 9781009551854 (HB), 9781009551809 (PB), 9781009551816 (OC)
ISSNs: 2635-232X (online), 2635-2311 (print)

Contents

Introduction

This Element introduces the reader to the phenomenon and problem of anticultism in France, with special attention to the history and present-day state of the Church of Scientology, which has been considered a quintessential example of a "cult" (or *secte*, which is the equivalent term in French) by anticultists. For decades, English-language scholarship has paid attention to the ways in which new religions or new religious movements (NRMs), which are two preferred and more neutral alternatives to the term "cults," have been subject to discrimination and persecution in France (see e.g., Beckford, 1981, 2004; Hervieu-Léger, 2001a, 2001b, 2004; Palmer, 2002, 2008, 2009, 2011; Duvert, 2004; Fautré, Garay, & Nidegger, 2004; Introvigne, 2004; Luca, 2004; Altglas, 2008; Willaime, 2010; Machi, 2013; Ollion, 2013; Garay, 2019; Adeliyan Tous, Richardson, & Taghipour, 2023; Westbrook, 2023). Typically, such works have examined, justifiably, the relationship between France's particular brand of secularism and church-state separation (*laïcité*) and the efforts of anticult initiatives, including those funded by the French state, with the most notable example being MIVILUDES (*Mission interministérielle de vigilance et de lutte contre les dérives sectaires*; Interministerial Mission of Vigilance and Combat against Cultic Deviance). That is to say, discussions of new religiosity in France are inevitably bound up with questions of politics, power, regulation, and the law.

France, of course, is by no means the only European country with a recent history of intolerance toward minority religions or NRMs. Germany, Russia, and Hungary stand out as examples among others (see e.g., Arweck & Clarke, 1997; Richardson, 2004; Máté-Tóth & Nagy, 2011, 2017; Richardson & Bellanger, 2014; Introvigne, 2014, 2017, 2018; Besier, 2017; Nilsson, 2017; Chryssides, 2019; Folk, 2019; Morton, 2020; Weightman, 2020; Miklovicz, 2021; Arjona, 2021; Šorytė, 2021a, 2022, 2023). What makes France relatively unique, indeed perplexing, is that it represents the paradoxical case of a western democratic nation that upholds the separation of church and state and individual religious liberty yet has run up a track record of antagonism toward new religious groups and minority religious communities. The treatment of Muslims is surely the most obvious and well-publicized example (Bowen, 2007, 2010), which has received renewed international attention in light of the 2024 Summer Olympics in Paris (Ables, 2023; Reuters, 2023), but new religions have been affected as well. For example, in their book on government raids on religious groups, Stuart A. Wright and Susan J. Palmer (2016) analyzed a variety of affected communities around the world (such as the Twelve Tribes, Branch Davidians, and Church of Scientology, among others). However, they dedicate an entire chapter on the history of raids on NRMs in France – the only country to receive this level of treatment. Within France, Wright and Palmer discovered that of all the new and alternative religious groups that have been raided by the state since the 1970s, the Church of Scientology, affiliated Scientology organizations, and individual Scientologists were targeted more than any other group (twenty-one raids between 1971 and 2008 alone by their count; Wright & Palmer, 2016, p. 218).[1] "In some cases," they explained, "we found that there were as many as ten simultaneous raids on members' homes in conjunction with raids on the Scientology Church or its offices." The authors continued, "Had we counted each raid on a residence, the numbers would have been much higher. It would be quite plausible to make the case that the actual number of police raids on Scientology/Scientologists in France was closer to 50" (Wright & Palmer, 2016, p. 221).

A focus on French anticultism and the Church of Scientology therefore makes historical and sociological as well as methodological sense. Indeed, an analysis of the history and situation of French Scientology is an ideal case study for situating the larger arc of anticultism in the country, especially since Scientologists have had a continued institutional presence in the country since the late 1950s. This approach with a focus on a single NRM also has the benefit of contributing to the academic study of Scientology outside of its origination points in the United States, by helping fill a lacuna that will hopefully encourage even more academic investigation, especially given the evident challenges for scholars of new religions in France. Bernadette Rigal-Cellard, one of the leading French scholars of new religions, has written powerfully about these obstacles in an article whose title speaks for itself: "'Do Not Dare Speak of Scientology in France!'" (2021). As Rigal-Cellard put it: "More so than any other minority religion, [Scientology] is held as THE tentacular cult that has infiltrated the major levels of government, the judicial system, and because of people like myself, the education networks" (2021, p. 182). "Consequently," she went on, "if you are a scholar of religions in France, you will not have the slightest problem studying Scientology *per se*, but you run the risk of being seriously attacked by not only the iconic anticult brigade but also by society at large, by mainstream media and possibly by your own institution" (Rigal-Cellard, 2021, p. 182; see also Šorytė, 2021b). In this intellectual climate, it is not altogether surprising that a great many academic studies of France and NRMs, including Scientology, have come from scholars working outside the country. This Element is no exception and stands on the shoulders of a great

---

[1] Palmer and Wright compiled data on numerous other NRM raids in France, for instance on the Raelians, ISKCON, Longo Maï, The Family International, Horus, Aumism/Mandarom, Twelve Tribes, Steiner/Waldorf schools, and Community of the Beatitudes, among others (2016, p. 200).

many researchers, operating both in and out of France, including James A. Beckford, Bernadette Rigal-Cellard, Régis Dericquebourg, James T. Richardson, Susan J. Palmer, Stuart A. Wright, Willy Fautré, Danièle Hervieu-Léger, Véronique Altglas, and Massimo Introvigne.

Section 1 of this Element provides an overview of anticultism in France, including the relationship between anticultism and modern French secularism (*laïcité*). Not only has France developed a culture of antagonism to *sectes* in ways that have expressed themselves legally and institutionally, but the country is the birthplace of the European-wide anticult network FECRIS (*Fédération Européenne des Centres de Recherche et d'Information sur le Sectarisme*; European Federation of Centres of Research and Information on Cults and Sects), founded in Paris in 1994 and now based in Marseille (FECRIS, 2024). A study of anticultism in France, therefore, offers a window into the problems and peculiarities of anticultism that exist elsewhere in Europe. At the same time, again illustrating the paradoxes at play, France is home to the European Court of Human Rights (ECtHR, in Strasbourg), which has at times served as a legal resource and counterbalance for French- and European-wide NRMs as they seek a voice and redress for discrimination and prejudice that may otherwise go unresolved or dismissed (see e.g., Richardson & Shoemaker, 2008; Fokas & Richardson, 2019; Adeliyan Tous, Richardson, & Taghipour, 2023). Much of Section 1 focuses on MIVILUDES, which receives state support, and the relevant example of Sonia Backès, a former Scientologist (who became a critic of the Church of Scientology) and who briefly held a cabinet position in the Borne-Macron government (2022–2023) that put MIVILUDES under her purview. It is argued that MIVILUDES represents an extreme, hardline, and activist expression of *laïcité*, one that is often unsupported elsewhere in the French government (and French society), where a comparably open-minded or tolerant form of *laïcité* reigns. This section makes use of material from interviews conducted with Scientologists, including Backès's stepfather. These were carried out during my first research trip to Paris and Brussels in early 2023. I conducted twenty-five formal interviews with members at the Church of Scientology Celebrity Centre (Paris) and another with a veteran Sea Org member at the Churches of Scientology for Europe campus (Brussels). A follow-up visit to Paris was carried out in September 2023, which allowed me to visit the Church of Scientology of Paris and explore the site of the Church of Scientology and Celebrity Centre of Greater Paris (Ideal Org) in Saint-Denis.

Section 2 examines as a case study the Church of Scientology, tracing its history and how it has arguably become the most prominent example of a so-called cult in France, as a result of the anti-Scientology propaganda of anti-cultists, MIVILUDES, and the media. This section draws even more extensively on my interviews with French Scientologists as well as archival research and, as with this work as a whole, is part of a larger and ongoing project on Scientology in France (see e.g., Westbrook, 2023; Introvigne, 2023d). Since this volume focuses attention on anticultism and its expressions and effects – for example, legally, culturally, socially, and so on – material relevant to this theme is emphasized in the selected interview data (as opposed to other possibilities, such as an emphasis on lived or ordinary religious life and the benefits members receive from Scientology services).

A third and concluding section offers reflections on the future of new and minority religions in France, especially with respect to recent legal issues. Finally, an Appendix is provided with a timeline of major dates in the history of French anticultism, with particular attention to Scientology.

1 From the Solar Temple to MIVILUDES: Anticultism in France, Past and Present

In France, as elsewhere, the history of anticultism can be demarcated by particular incidents, the passing of seminal or controversial laws, or reactions of individuals (or the state) to particular groups and their beliefs or practices. In the United States, for instance, the tragedy of the murders/suicides at Jonestown in 1978 represented a paradigm shift – one that resulted in societal fears about the dangers of so-called "cults" – and in France perhaps the closest parallel came in the form of the murders/suicides associated with the Order of the Solar Temple (1994–1995, 1997). The Solar Temple incidents of the 1990s, as other researchers have acknowledged (Introvigne, 2000; Mayer, 2006; Palmer, 2011, p. 9), resulted in anticult backlashes, conflations, and fears of similar possibilities, most prominently, in France, with the calling of a Parliamentary Commission on Sectes, held in July 1995, that was followed by similar legislative commissions, for instance in 1999 and 2006. In December 1995, the French National Assembly first released its Guyard Report, as it has come to be known, which, among other items, listed 173 cultic groups and movements, including a number of well-known NRMs such as the Church of Scientology, Unification Movement, International Raelian Movement, Twelve Tribes, and International Society for Krishna Consciousness (ISKCON), but also others, such as Evangelical Christian and Buddhist groups. Since its release, the Guyard Report has been heavily criticized, both inside and outside of France, including in an anthology coedited by NRM scholars Massimo Introvigne and J. Gordon Melton (1996). The anticult group MIVILUDES now maintains that there is no official list of *sectes* in France and that this earlier inventory is outdated and lacks utility. However, the public relations damage of the Guyard Report has arguably been done. In many cases, the groups targeted in France by the late 1990s either no longer exist or have had their operations significantly curtailed. Indeed, the two largest NRMs still operating in France today are both American-born imports: the Jehovah's Witnesses and the Church of Scientology.

Although the Order of the Solar Temple tragedy and Guyard Report are significant in charting the recent history of anticultism in France – and may well, in fact, represent sociological and legal powder keg moments (Mayer, 2006, p. 17) – it would be misleading and reductionistic to view them as the exclusive causes for the state-sponsored monitoring of *sectes* that has arisen in the last quarter century. An inordinate focus on them would also ignore the preexistence of *secte*-watching organizations, such as ADFI (*Association de défense des familles et de l'individu*, Association for the Defense of Families and the Individual; founded in 1974), CCMM (*Centre contre les manipulations mentales*, Center Against Mind Control; founded in 1981), UNADFI (*Union nationale des associations de défense des familles et de l'individu*, the National Union of Associations for the Defense of Families and the Individual; founded in 1982 as an organizing body for the ADFI chapters across France), and FECRIS (founded in 1994 in Paris), the last of which is now based in Marseille but coordinates a network of affiliated organizations across Europe under its "umbrella" (Arweck, 2006, p. 115). The anticult influence of FECRIS within and beyond France has been analyzed (and scrutinized) by NRM scholars as well as human rights activists (see e.g., Besier & Seiwert, 2012; Dericquebourg, 2012; Berzano, et al., 2022a, 2022b; Introvigne, 2023e) – and it should be noted that 90 percent of FECRIS's budget comes from the French government (Duval, 2018). Focusing on the Solar Temple and Guyard Report would also fail to properly take into account the cumulative influence in French society of anti-*secte* publications and critical media coverage, some of which are listed in the appendix timeline at the end of this work or discoverable in the bibliography. One example is the 1983 publication of *Les sectes en France* by Alain Vivien. This work was commissioned by Prime Minister Pierre Mauroy and established the concept of *secte absolue* (absolute cult) to refer to the most harmful and dangerous groups in France – a label, for instance, applied to Scientology by Vivien. Vivien would later become director of MILS (*Mission Interministérielle de Lutte contre les Sectes*, Interministerial Mission to Combat Cults), a precursor to the present-day MIVILUDES. And of course, a focus on recent anticult history in France would be incomplete without an understanding of legal history and precedent – extending as far back as the 1789 Declaration of the Rights of Man and of the Citizen as Véronique Altglas has observed (2010, p. 495) – and extending into the early twentieth century with laws regarding associations (1901) and the separation of church and state (1905) and into the twenty-first century with legislation such as the controversial About-Picard Law of 2001 and the role of "mental manipulation" in so-called cultic movements.

Paradoxically, France is also home to the European Court of Human Rights (ECtHR) of the Council of Europe in Strasbourg. The ECtHR has served as a counterbalancing judicial force in response to human rights violations, including in the area of freedom of religion or belief (FORB), not only across France but elsewhere on the continent, as explored by James T. Richardson and others (Fokas & Richardson, 2019; Adeliyan Tous, Richardson, & Taghipour, 2023). However, challenges certainly remain within France, including at the level of state-sponsored forms of anticultism, with MIVILUDES as the most obvious and antagonistic expression of anti-*secte* informed *laïcité* (state secularism) in the country as of this writing. An investigation of MIVILUDES – past and present – in turn reveals the essential historical and legal context for some of the institutional difficulties faced by minority religious groups such as the Church of Scientology, as explored later in this section and especially in Section 2.

MIVILUDES, the French government's agency to monitor and combat "cultic/sectarian deviances" (*dérives sectaires*) (MIVILUDES, 2023a), was formed in 2002, in the wake of a previous and similar but even more militant group, MILS, which was inaugurated in 1998. Susan Palmer (2011) has unpacked and analyzed the history of MIVILUDES and its predecessors, which operate with state funding that trickles down to affiliated countercult and anticult organizations, including UNADFI and CCMM. Anti-*secte* (i.e., anticult) presumptions about new or alternative groups are often predicated on ideas about mind control and brainwashing that have long been criticized as exaggerated and misleading, if not outright pseudoscientific, such as the work of French anticult psychiatrist Jean-Marie Abgrall (Abgrall, 2002; Anthony & Robbins, 2004), but the conflation of *secte*, cult, and mind control continues to influence popular perception about religious minorities (see e.g., Introvigne, 2022a). Moreover, even though the French government's *de jure* separation of Church and State prevents it from deciding whether or not an organization is a bona fide religion, much less a *secte* (a term, incidentally, with no legal definition in France), this has not stopped MIVILUDES from singling out particular groups in its annual reports. In its report for 2021, for instance, the Church of Scientology and the Jehovah's Witnesses are jointly discussed in a section as examples of "multinationals of spirituality" (*multinationales de la spiritualité*) (MIVILUDES, 2022, pp. 58–71), as evidence of French suspicions about foreign ideological influences such as these two American-born religious traditions (see e.g., Kaiser, 1994; Luca & Lenoir, 1998; Introvigne, 2023b,

2023c). On the one hand, the absence of an explicit list of designated *sectes/* cults, such as those put out by the controversial Guyard Report in 1995, might seem like a sign of improvement for religious minorities in France. On the other hand, it might be interpreted as an implicit sign of the success of anticult organizations such as MIVILUDES, UNADFI, and CCMM given that many of those same groups no longer formally exist in the country or have dwindled in numbers to the point of obscurity and irrelevance. As Wright and Palmer put it in their work on government raids on religious communities, "the [French] state has the power to drive many *sectes* out of business, underground, or out of the country with impunity. So in the final analysis, France's 'War on Sects' may simply be a war of attrition" (2016, p. 224).

This war of attrition requires funding from the government to continue. For a number of years, especially in the late 2010s, it seemed as though MIVILUDES's influence was beginning to wane, particularly in the face of French concerns about Islamic terrorism (Bowen, 2007, 2010). Since mid-2021, however, MIVILUDES seems to have been resurrected and is set to "experience a revival of sort," with 1 million euros per year secured in state funding (Duval, 2021), which can be distributed to anticult associations such as UNADFI and CCMM. The reasons for this recent infusion of financial lifeblood into MIVILUDES seem at least partially bound up with responses to misinformation in the wake of the COVID-19 pandemic and efforts to vaccinate the French public. The MIVILUDES website, for instance, devotes much attention to health and alternative medicine (MIVILUDES, 2023b). In a recent annual report, an introduction authored by Sonia Backès (a former Scientologist and politician in the Macron government who then had MIVILUDES under her purview, to be discussed at greater length in this section) noted the following: "Cultic phenomena deliberately undermine the freedom of conscience and the integrity of individuals. The health crisis has certainly been fertile ground for these movements. . . . By calling into question the science and the credibility of health authorities, these discourses jeopardize public health" (MIVILUDES, 2022, p. 7). Again, the Church of Scientology and the Jehovah's Witnesses are arguably the two largest and most resilient of the remaining so-called cults in France; they both have received criticisms for their alleged views on science and health, and they both enjoy funding and institutional support from headquarters in the United States (and a membership spread around the world). Scientologists have also been instrumental in fostering interfaith efforts, especially among other new or minority religions, both in France and around the world, to raise awareness about persecution, religious freedom, and human rights. Scientology spokesperson and interfaith leader Éric Roux is perhaps the most visible representative of the Church of Scientology in France and Europe more broadly. In addition to a growing body of popular and scholarly work (see e.g., Roux, 2012, 2014, 2017, 2018, 2021a, 2021b), he has encouraged open dialogue between Scientologists and French Freemasons (Roux, 2019), who are traditionally among the most vocal secular critics of religion in general and Scientology in particular. In 2022, for example, he fostered dialogue with the Druze at Scientology's European headquarters in Brussels (Churches of Scientology for Europe, 2022) in addition to dozens of other religious groups. Also in 2022, Roux was elected as the Global Council Trustee for Europe at the United Religions Initiative (URI), the first Scientologist to hold this position, and he joined the Executive Committee of this large international organization the following year (URI, 2023).

Despite interfaith progress and institutional resilience among NRMs such as Scientology and Jehovah's Witnesses, the resurgence of anticultism in France represented by MIVILUDES poses a threat to not only minority religions but also other individuals and groups that are deemed problematic from the standpoint of public health and social welfare. On my trip to Paris in early 2023, I learned that MIVILUDES has begun to target nonreligious groups, including homeopathic practitioners and vaccination critics, in the wake of the COVID-19 pandemic, which makes sense in light of its attention to public health and alternative medicine. But MIVILUDES continues to target alleged "cultic deviances" or abuses in religious settings, with, as mentioned, Scientology and the Jehovah's Witnesses as the two largest organizations in its sights. In 2021, the French government even republished an old graphic novel, *Dans la Secte* (*In the Cult*), which follows a young woman allegedly recruited into Scientology in the 1980s, implying once again that this group represents the quintessential example of a *secte* in France (Guillon & Alloing, 2021). The same work, remarkably, was distributed by MIVILUDES to an astonishing 11,000 school libraries (Centers of Documentation and Information) in France during the pandemic (Claude, 2022), with the support of a budget of 85,000 euros from the government's Interministerial Fund for the Prevention of Delinquency (*Fonds interministériel de prévention de la délinquance*).[2]

In Paris, I spoke with a Scientologist who is also an attorney on behalf of the church in France (and who has represented many other religious minorities, including internationally). He offered the following perspective on MIVILUDES and its mission:

---

[2] Freedom of Information document, provided to the author by Éric Roux, received on November 18, 2021 from the Interministerial Fund for the Prevention of Delinquency (reference number: 2021/FIPD/Radicalisation_065).

[MILS] changed their name into MIVILUDES, which is not supposed to fight against religious entities, but against abuses. . . . Honestly, in practice, it's not true. It's still the same [as MILS]. It's still presuming that some organizations are dangerous and then they target [them]. . . . The MIVILUDES is a kind of anticult, anti-religious organization even if they don't say they are. They say they are fighting against abuses ... everybody agrees to fight against abuse. . . . I agree also to fight against abuse, but the point is that the definition of abuse is corresponding to the religious practice. That's not OK because France is a secular state. There is a separation between the Church, historically, and the State. There is freedom of religion, of course, in the constitution. We should not have an organization within the government fighting against abuse because there is a common law which is equal for everybody. . . . If there is abuse in any religious entity, that's a common law. You should prosecute it, and that's all. . . . There is no need for a specific entity or a specific law to fight against abuse that can happen in any religion. There are abuse[s] sometimes in some religion[s] but that doesn't mean that you have to fight the religious entity itself or the religion itself. That's what they [MIVILUDES] are doing, in fact. They are not supposed to do it officially, but they do it.[3]

In addition to pointing out MIVILUDES's history of targeting religious groups themselves instead of alleged abuses, this Scientologist noted what he described as a "schizophrenic" state of affairs within the Ministry of Home Affairs, which houses both MIVILUDES to fight abuses as well as the Bureau of Religious Denominations (*Bureau des Cultes*) to monitor relations between the State and major or mainline religious bodies. The existence of these entities might appear quite perplexing and even at odds with Article 1 of the French Constitution: "France shall be an indivisible, secular, democratic and social Republic. It shall ensure the equality of all citizens before the law, without distinction of origin, race or religion. It shall respect all beliefs" (French National Assembly, 2019). But it soon enough becomes clear that freedom of religion in France does not imply, strictly speaking, a complete or entirely clear separation of Church and State. The full legal origins and history of French *laïcité* (state secularism) are outside the scope of this project (see e.g., Baubérot, 1999, 2014, 2021; Haarscher, 2021), but it is worth mentioning some historical background to help better understand the curious place of a body such as MIVILUDES in France today. Since the French government does not officially or legally recognize particular religions per its 1905 Law on the Separation of the Churches and State (*Loi du 9 décembre 1905 concernant la séparation des Églises et de l'État*), religious groups are technically organized and regarded as *associations* (Baubérot, 2014, p. 101; Dericquebourg, 2017). This, in turn, was built on a 1901 law

---

[3] Interview with French Scientologist, Paris, January 28, 2023. Name withheld.

guaranteeing freedom of associations more generally (Haarscher, 2021, p. 20).[4] So, in theory, state secularism, or *laïcité*, is intended to function as a safeguard against a state-sponsored and state-subsidized Church (namely the Catholic Church, historically) and guarantee freedom of religious practices for all French citizens.[5] In practice, though, especially in light of new and minority religious groups making their way to France in the second half of the twentieth century, nontraditional groups have been singled out and marginalized. Some subsidies and other financial benefits remain for older churches (funneled through their "cultural association" legal status), in particular those with a presence in the country prior to 1905. This confusing state of affairs has been exacerbated by incidents such as the Solar Temple murders/suicides and the Guyard Report (see Introvigne & Melton, 1996). Indeed, it was the Guyard Report that planted the seeds for the rise of the Interministerial Observatory on Sects (created May 1996), which was replaced two years later, in 1998, by MILS and then resurrected yet again, in 2002, in the form of MIVILUDES (Palmer, 2011, pp. 9–21). In June 2001, the controversial About-Picard Law was passed. It empowered the work of anticult activists by lending legal legitimacy to ideas connected to what, in English, are referred to as brainwashing psychological theories (Palmer, 2011, pp. 21–2) – notions that, once again, are disputed or dismissed out of hand as pseudoscientific by many researchers (see e.g., Anthony & Robbins, 2004; Introvigne, 2022a).

MIVILUDES came up frequently in my interviews in Paris with Scientologists. They were concerned about its support from the state, legally and financially, and the threat it poses to religious liberty for all French citizens and not merely the Church of Scientology.[6] "I'm not sure they [MIVILUDES] have a lot of support," one Scientologist told me, reflecting on the group more generally within society. "Even I believe some people in the government don't really think it's so useful," this member continued. "I don't know. The problem is that in France, let's say if [the] government gives less money to MIVILUDES, then you will have a campaign of the press to say, we don't do enough against the cults and everything. . . . It's [a] tricky situation." Another echoed this sentiment and added that funding to MIVILUDES means uninterrupted funding for affiliated organizations: "You have all these other

---

[4] Notably, Scientology centers are organized as associations under *both* the 1901 and 1905 laws, per Éric Roux, a complexity that I missed in my earlier study of Scientology in France (2023). For more on French Scientology associations in relation to the 1905 law, see Pansier (2018, 2022).

[5] The full extent of the complex relationship between French Catholicism, minority religion, and *laïcité* is relevant but outside the scope of this Element. For more, see Beckford (2004), Kuru (2009, pp. 136–58), Introvigne, et al. (2020), and Davis (2020).

[6] Quotations in this section are drawn from interviews with French Scientologists in Paris, January 2023.

associations [e.g., UNADFI, CCMM] who can only live through MIVILUDES. If there is no MIVILUDES, they don't exist anymore." Others in my sample noted that MIVILUDES has shifted its focus in recent years, particularly in the wake of the COVID-19 pandemic, away from minority religious groups and onto alternative medical practices. "[MIVILUDES is now] against all these doctors ... alternative medicine," one Scientologist said. "They're attacking that now because they have finished with the cults. Now they're attacking individuals or doctors." Another agreed but pointed out that groups such as Scientology certainly remain on its radar. "I think the government ... [is] pushing to show that we have [a] 'secte' in France, we have Scientology, we have alternative medicine [practices] which are 'not good,' which are dangerous," as he put it, suggesting a push to conflate popular perceptions about *sectes* with other groups, such as anti-vaxxers and critics of mainstream medical practices and public health recommendations. (During my 2023 trips to Paris, I should add, Scientologists were still mindful of COVID public health protocols and, on my first trip in early 2023, I was required to use a hand sanitizer and have my forehead temperature taken before proceeding to the rest of the church building where interviews were conducted.)

Despite other targets and a rhetoric of opposition to abuse or mind control rather than groups per se, it seems clear to me that MIVILUDES and its leaders are indeed opposed to Scientology's presence and expansion in the country. This explains, for instance, concern about the April 2024 opening of a new Saint-Denis church. As far as I can tell, MIVILUDES does not have direct or unilateral legal authority to prevent the opening or operation of a new Scientology church, but it certainly promotes fear of groups such as Scientology by publicly labeling and describing them under the umbrella of *sectes*. Wright and Palmer have written at length about government raids on religious communities, including an entire chapter on raids in France (2016, pp. 198–24). "The mere complaint by family of Scientology members, ex-members, journalists, or staff of MIVILUDES (or other ACM [anticult movement] organizations)," the coauthors found, "has been sufficient to trigger government raids" (2016, p. 217) and by their count there were an astounding twenty-one raids on Scientology churches and affiliated centers between 1971 and 2009 (2016, p. 218). As of late 2023, the French state now also has the power to make use of "special investigation techniques," a euphemism that would allow police to view mail and email, plant listening devices in homes, and even impersonate "cult" members, among other covert tactics, in order "to facilitate the work of investigators in the combat against the cultic deviances" (Introvigne, 2023a; French Republic, 2023). In such a state-supported anticult milieu, it is not at all surprising – on the contrary, it is arguably even predictable – that the Church of Scientology would encounter at least some pushback and setbacks in its goals for organizational expansion. In Saint-Denis, for instance, the mayor and other local officials initially opposed Scientology to such an extent that they temporarily halted construction of the new "Ideal Org" – a tactic that ultimately failed when the Paris Administrative Court of Appeal intervened in late 2021 and declared it a "misuse of power" on the part of the municipality and the State (*Le Figaro*, 2021; US Department of State, 2021). In a message to the church, Scientology leader David Miscavige announced the opening of this new French center (described online as an "Ideal Church of Scientology and Celebrity Centre") that finally took place on April 6, 2024 (Church of Scientology International, 2023c).

One recent and vocal opponent of Scientology in France was Sonia Backès (b. 1976), a second-generation (ex-)Scientologist, who served in the French government as Secretary of State for Citizenship (a status below minister in the French government) from mid-2022 to late 2023. This meant that MIVILUDES fell under Secretary Backès's purview. Backès is not new to French politics and has been active as an organizer and official from New Caledonia, a French colony, since the early 2000s, until she lost a senatorial race in late 2023 that led to her resignation from the Macron government (and with it, her supervision over MIVILUDES) (Fisher, 2023; Menu, 2023). I can find no evidence that Secretary Backès ever spoke out against, or even about, Scientology in her public life prior to assuming this position (and, even then, only after the July 2022 death of her mother, who was a longtime Scientologist). Italian NRM scholar Massimo Introvigne interviewed Backès's brother, who claimed that his sister was motivated to speak out against Scientology for political reasons, in particular out of fear that the media would reveal their mother's identity as a Scientologist. As the brother described to Introvigne:

> Well, a few days before she died, my mother showed and gave me a text message that Sonia had just sent to her. In the text message, Sonia was explaining that she was going to have MIVILUDES in her portfolio as a State Secretary, and that she was afraid that Mediapart (a French online newspaper specialized in investigating politicians and potential scandals) would discover that our mother was a Scientologist. As you know, MIVILUDES has always promoted the discrimination of Scientologists. Then, Sonia added that for this reason, she would have to say that she had left the family because of Scientology, to avoid a scandal. My mother answered that, instead of inventing stories, she should tell the truth, which is that she always respected the religion of her family and was in fact respecting the freedom of religion of anyone, and that would have been it. The truth is that she never attacked the chosen religion of her mother, stepfather, and brother until she got a government position in relation with the MIVILUDES, where it is expected that she is a bigot. (Introvigne, 2022b)

On my first research trip to Paris in January 2023 (Westbrook, 2023), I interviewed Backès's stepfather, Joël Laplantif, a medical doctor and longtime Scientologist in Paris who for decades was married to Backès's mother – and who has known his stepdaughter since she was six years old. The stepfather corroborated the account of the brother and filled in a number of other details, all supported by evidence such as photographs, text message screenshots, and other documents that were provided to me. These text messages (dated July 10, 2022) indeed support the brother's assertions to Introvigne, but even more revealing, I think, is the way in which Backès begins to self-consciously reimagine her past association with Scientology for explicitly political purposes. Based on reading through the text messages, my view is that Backès was indeed concerned about negative media coverage due to her mother's membership in the Church of Scientology – presumably an unacceptable liability given the new political role that put her over MIVILUDES. At the same time, she and her mother were apparently on good terms (Figure 1), planning to see one another in the near future. Backès even invited her mother and stepfather to her new office in July 2022 to help celebrate the new position. In addition, there are photographs and a video of Backès and her Scientologist family members dining, smiling, and even singing together, up to mid-2022. In the months

Figure 1 Sonia Backès (center) with her mother (left) and stepfather (right). Paris, April 2022. Courtesy of Joël Laplantif.

after her mother's death in late July 2022, Backès put forward a number of specific claims about her Scientology involvement and disaffiliation that the stepfather disputed during our interview. After reviewing Backès's claims, and the stepfather and brother's counterclaims, it appeared to me that Backès should be analyzed as more of an "ordinary leave-taker" or perhaps a "defector," and certainly an "invisible former member," who, by the second half of 2022, began to publicly fashion a solidly antagonistic, disaffected, and vocal "apostate" narrative, to borrow from the typologies developed by Bromley and Introvigne (see e.g., Bromley, 1998; Introvigne, 1999, pp. 83–5).

As of this writing, Backès has not published a memoir, unlike some other vocal critics of Scientology (see e.g., Cusack, 2020; Melton & Ashcraft, 2021, pp. 80–2), but has nonetheless given enough information to various media outlets that a basic timeline and narrative of her involvement (and disaffiliation) can be assembled. My interview with the stepfather and Introvigne's interview with the brother reveal a number of claims and counterclaims. On the one hand, her claims illustrate a rhetorical strategy that relies heavily on anticult tropes about alienation, susceptibility, mind control, and so on, which would communicate effectively and alarmingly to French audiences fearful of *sectes*. On the other hand, counterclaims from the stepfather call this narrative into question and also arguably showcase L. Ron Hubbard's strategy in public relations to "dead agent" false information – i.e., to prove untrue – a phrase taken from Sun Tzu's *The Art of War* (Hubbard, 1972; Westbrook, 2018, p. 382).

Backès claims, for instance, that her mother first became interested in Scientology in the early 1980s after filling out a personality test that preyed on her "vulnerability . . . in the middle of a divorce" (BFMTV, 2022; see also Tervé, 2022). However, according to her stepfather, "The divorce was ended [in] August 1982, and we met [in] Scientology in 1984," and both of them freely and actively participated in church life for more than three decades. Backès also claims that she attended a "Scientology school" at the age of nine, where her mother was a director, and was subjected to a "form of lie detector" (Boichot, 2022; France Info, 2022). In reality, the educational center was, and she has even clarified as much, the Paris-based "School of Awakening," which was indeed run by Scientologists (including her mother) and made use of Hubbard's educational (Study Technology) methods, as do other schools around the world (see e.g., Frisk, 2018) and which was open to non-Scientologists as well. The School of Awakening was "closed down by the state. . . .fortunately," in Backès's estimation (BFMTV, 2022). In another interview, she claimed: "The School of Awakening was shut down and I joined a traditional public school. It was the action of the public authorities that saved me" (Adenor, 2022). But in fact, the school was not closed by the state at this time, as implied in interviews, and continued to function for at least another ten years (the school was located at 11 Passage Courtois in Paris and operated from the early 1980s to 1997), long after Backès was put back in the public school system by her mother. The "lie detector" in question is of course a simplistic reference to the E-Meter, which in educational contexts can sometimes be used for "word clearing" purposes (i.e., defining and ensuring the understanding of words and phrases), as explained by the stepfather, a distinction not at all emphasized in Backès's self-presentation.

Secretary Backès has also spoken about when, at the age of twelve, her mother sent her "to London in the European HQ" of Scientology, "when I started to doubt … and that's where I threw everything away" (BFMTV, 2022), eventually hitchhiking her way out of England. According to the step-father, the reality is far less sensational. Backès went to Scientology's Saint Hill center – which is in East Grinstead, not London – to take an introductory course, "Personal Values and Integrity," but soon after decided to stop and leave. Her mother and stepfather then paid her way to fly home to France. Eventually, with the mother's consent, Backès chose to live with her biological father in New Caledonia. "We respected her decision. Since she decided not to keep going with Scientology, no problem," recalled the stepfather, who added that he paid for the cost of the flights for Backès to return to New Caledonia. Finally, Backès has insinuated that leaving the Church of Scientology led to estrangement from family members who were still members. "My mother remained a Scientologist until her death. … My mother lives quite far from me so I didn't see her often," as she put it in one interview (BFMTV, 2022). However, according to the stepfather, the mother and daughter maintained good communication, even after she left the Church of Scientology and moved on with her life. The mother and stepfather paid for Backès's university studies and housing, and even vacationed together on numerous occasions. On one such trip to Florida in 1999 – according to the stepfather, years after leaving Scientology behind in England – Backès even visited Clearwater, home of Scientology's international Flag Land Base, and met with a Scientologist friend visiting from Paris. In fact, Backès went so far as stating that after leaving France for New Caledonia in 1990 that she did not see her mother for several years. "I refused to see my mother again for a very long time, for several years," she claimed in a March 2023 television program (France 2, 2023). However, the stepfather showed photographs of Backès with her mother from 1990 to 1993 and in subsequent years.

From the stepfather's perspective, Backès's revised history is evidence that she is a "compulsive liar" and "1.1" (Scientology jargon for covertly hostile). But he also places blame on MIVILUDES and a political culture that he believes forced her to adopt an anti-Scientology position for political survival. "She was really under the enforced decision from MIVILUDES and the guys behind [it]," according to the stepfather. "She thinks she has power and immunity. ... I think she is the village puppet of this kind of person behind the scene." Whatever the personal or political motivations at play, what is clear is that Backès also emerged as a vocal opponent of the Saint-Denis Ideal Org project, saying in a January 2023 interview that "we need new tools to prohibit this" (Négroni, 2023). In a March 2023 editorial in *Le Figaro*, Backès emphasized the need for a "change of scale" in the state's fight against sectarian (cultic) deviance (Backès, 2023) and once again situated MIVILUDES's mission in the context of public health. "To the multinationals of spirituality which continue to rage, such as the Jehovah's Witnesses or the Church of Scientology," Backès wrote, "are now added a myriad of movements and individuals who invest particularly in the fields of health, food and well-being" (Backès, 2023). She also announced her plan to "organize the first national meetings for the fight against cultic deviances. They will bring together the relevant State services, institutional partners, members of Parliament, the Government, representatives of associations as well as European and national actors, experts and qualified personalities" (Backès, 2023). This resulted in a "National Conference on Combating Cultic Deviances" in 2023 (Introvigne, 2023d). What exactly these developments – and reinvigorated anti-Scientology political posture – hold for the future of the Church of Scientology in France, including its new center in Saint-Denis, remains to be seen.

In the end, perhaps what truly makes Backès's apostate narrative unique is her background as a second-generation (former) Scientologist (i.e., a former *secte* member) and the relatively brief but remarkable position of political power she wielded. Her brief tenure showcased the ability to damage her (former) religion – for instance, by speaking out to the media, shaping public policy and action through MIVILUDES, and, perhaps most pointedly, voicing opposition to the new Ideal Org in Saint-Denis. Moreover, Backès emerged, in effect, as a *second-generation political anti-Scientologist*, a category that has not been well enough examined in the literature, at least with respect to Scientology, apostasy, and disaffiliation. To be sure, critics of Scientology have run for (and even won) political office in Los Angeles, California or Clearwater, Florida on platforms that featured anti-Scientology messages (Haskell, 2022). In Backès's case, though, the situation is quite different. Again, she publicly emerged as a second-generation disgruntled ex-Scientologist only *after* assuming a position with oversight of MIVILUDES, the very organization responsible for monitoring groups such as Scientology. As new religious groups like the Church of Scientology have grown up in the twentieth century, the rise of multiple generations of members (and former members) demographically paved the way for someone like Backès, suggesting the possibility that similar career paths – at the intersection of public life and anticult activism – might emerge for other second-generation NRM members. Time will tell.

2 The Most Dangerous Foreign *Secte*? A Brief History of Scientology Persecution (and Resilience) in France

The Church of Scientology's presence (and social and legal persecution) in France has already been taken up at some length in the academic literature, for instance, by Susan Palmer (2002, 2008, 2009, 2011), Stuart Wright (Wright & Palmer, 2016), Bernadette Rigal-Cellard (2019, 2021), Régis Dericquebourg (1998a, 1998b, 1998c, 2000, 2001, 2011), and Nathalie Luca (2004), among others, publishing both in English and French.[7] However, not surprisingly, the bulk of the material published on Scientology in French approaches the subject from the anti-*secte* (i.e., anticult) perspective, and researchers searching for an inventory of this critical body of work over the decades (e.g., from ex-members, journalists, psychologists, and anticult activists) will find no shortage of such works in the references list (see e.g., Woodrow, 1977; Petit-Castelli, 1979; d'Eaubonne, 1982; Morin, 1982; Pasquini, 1993; Ranc, 1993; Fouchereau, 1996; Lenzini, 1996; Ariès, 1998, 1999; Darcondo, 1998; Champion & Cohen, 1999).

Institutionally, the Church of Scientology in France traces its origins to 1959, when on October 26 the Friends of Scientology association was formed. One of the earliest pioneers in France was Mario Feninger, a French–Egyptian classical pianist I happened to interview in Los Angeles more than a decade ago in preparation for my first book, *Among the Scientologists* (Westbrook, 2019). In that interview, Feninger claimed, rightly so, to be the "founder of the Paris organization" (Westbrook, 2019, p. 64), which was corroborated in a separate interview carried out with him by Scientology staff member Éric Roux, now Vice President of the Church of Scientology's European Office for Public Affairs and Human Rights. Following Feninger's death in 2016, I had the opportunity to attend his memorial service at the Church of Scientology Celebrity Centre International (Hollywood), where his early organizing efforts and influence, both in and outside of France, were acknowledged by friends and colleagues. Feninger's involvement can actually be traced back all the way to 1950, when an American friend gave him a copy of L. Ron Hubbard's

---

[7] The work of sociologist Roland Chagnon (1983, 1987) in Montréal also deserves mention, in particular *La Scientologie: Une Nouvelle Religion de la Puissance* (Scientology: A New Religion of Power) (1985).

Dianetics: The Modern Science of Mental Health (1950, 2007). *Dianetics* seems to have appealed to Feninger because just a year earlier, in 1949, he had studied general semantics in the United States under Alfred Korzybski, a figure acknowledged by Hubbard as one influence, among others, on Dianetics (see Hubbard, 1951).

Another important and early pioneer in early 1950s France was an American named John M. "Jack" Campbell (Figure 2),[8] who for years lived in Paris. Campbell was involved in the promotion of *Dianetics* in France several years before the first Scientology organization developed in 1959. This is revealed in a series of letters between L. Ron Hubbard and Campbell. For example, Campbell wrote to Hubbard about the successes of group processing (auditing), discussed translations of Scientology materials into French, and referred in more than one instance to a "Salon de Scientologie," as he put it, operating in Paris (June 1, 1955; November 5, 1956). In another letter to Hubbard, dated January 1, 1955, Campbell reflected on some of the early students and preclears of Scientology in France and challenges: "Interesting crowd: A physiologist, a teacher, a student, the rest artists and writers. They talk a bit of existentialism. In thinkingness they find it rather difficult to discriminate between Scientology and existentialism (like Dianetics/Scientology in the old days); in actual processing the confusion vanishes. We mostly process [i.e., audit]." In another letter to Hubbard, dated March 11, 1956, Campbell listed "Bishop of Paris" as his title. In a letter from Hubbard to Campbell, dated January 3, 1956, Hubbard – who by this point, it should be remembered, had founded Scientology churches

Figure 2 John M. "Jack" Campbell (left) and Alain Frank Rosenberg (right). Paris, 1980. Courtesy of Éric Roux.

---

[8] Not to be confused with John *W.* Campbell, the longtime editor of *Astounding Science Fiction* and a staunch early supporter of Hubbard's Dianetics movement.

in the United States in 1953 and 1954 – noted that "with reference to your questions on a popular introduction of a first book, you want 'Scientology, Modern Science of Ability,' a rewrite of Book One [i.e., *Dianetics: The Modern Science of Mental Health*]. Use American Edition of Book One to show."[9] This letter provides a glimpse into Campbell's coordination of early book promotion, with Hubbard's blessing and guidance, as well as other themes such as the transition from Dianetics to Scientology and how best to present the material to a French audience when French language materials were limited or still in development. Following the 1959 registration of the first Paris Scientology association, which was based out of an apartment, Feninger and Campbell took the lead in planting and growing Scientology in the ensuing decades. Feninger also spearheaded the delivery of lectures and courses in the Paris organization's early history. For instance, Marc Bromberg, a French Sea Org member based in Brussels whose own involvement with Scientology traces to 1967, recalled in an interview that in "the first course of Mario [Feninger] ... my wife and I, we were there. We didn't know anything about Scientology. Nothing at all." Feninger's powerful presentation, including Scientology's techniques for communication and personal efficiency, appealed to Bromberg so much that he and his wife soon after became actively involved in the organization. The impact of this introduction left an indelible impression. They served as Church of Scientology executives in a number of capacities, before Bromberg joined the Sea Org in 1993 (Figure 3). "I realized during this first lecture that Scientology could give me the [means ...] to call things exactly by their true name," Bromberg remembered, "which would get me out of any confusion about life. ... [T]hat's the basic reason why I became a Scientologist ... the truth about you without any justification, nothing, just the pure truth."[10]

Scientology's legal existence as a French association morphed several times in the 1960s and 1970s, as it did elsewhere around the world, including in the United States, where Hubbard's churches expanded and evolved in numerous ways before the adoption of a more uniform corporate structure in the early 1980s under the umbrella of the Church of Scientology International (Los Angeles). In France, another Scientology organization, the Hubbard Association of French Scientologists, was founded on December 27, 1968 and housed in another apartment in Paris. Bromberg vividly recalled reading a telegram, sent to the French association directly from L. Ron Hubbard, in July 1968: "The telegram said, 'The mission of Scientology of Paris is

---

[9] A copy of this letter was provided from Church of Scientology archives by Éric Roux and corroborated by an identical print copy found in the private library of Edward E. Marsh in Rosarito, Mexico.

[10] Interview with Marc Bromberg, Brussels, January 31, 2023.

Figure 3 Marc Bromberg (right of banner) and fellow Scientologists protesting
a legal case in Marseille. The banner, in English, reads: "Scientology: Forty
Years in France, A New Religion That Will Always Be There."
September 1999. Reuters/Bridgeman Images.

becoming officially a Scientology organization."[11] This was followed by the
founding of the Church of Scientology of France on April 26, 1971, and then
the French Association of Scientology on December 22, 1975. Notably, not all
Scientology associations in French history have carried the name
"Scientology," such as the "Church of New Understanding" and
"Association for the Study of the New Faith" (both dating to August 1977).
In the United States, too, there had been experiments with other names, such
as the 1953 founding of churches of "American Science" and "Spiritual
Engineering," but these quickly fell out of use (Westbrook, 2019, p. 85;
2022, p. 48). The French associations of "New Understanding" and "New
Faith," by contrast, arrived more than two decades after Hubbard had decided
on the name Scientology, and the motivation appears to have been guided by
legal and public relations factors in France by the late 1970s. "The name of
Scientology was not legally welcome," Marc Bromberg explained to me. "We
had been accused and we had been convicted," namely in a 1978 case that led
to the conviction of several executives, who were finally absolved on appeal

---

[11] A "mission" is a smaller Scientology center, whereas an "organization" (org) is traditionally
larger, has more staff members, and offers a wider range of Dianetics and Scientology services.

(*Le Monde*, 1980, 1981, 1997), thus helping explain the use of other names to avoid negative public attention for members and activities in France.

In October 1993, the Internal Revenue Service (IRS) in the United States granted American Scientology organizations tax-exempt status. The legal victory was celebrated by the Church of Scientology's ecclesiastical leader, David Miscavige, in an announcement now known internally as "The War is Over Event" (Urban, 2011, p. 173; Westbrook, 2019, pp. 176–7). One of my French interviewees attended in person and offered an instructive international perspective. This Scientologist, and a number of others with her, was heavily jetlagged from the flight to the United States, and she was put in charge of translating Miscavige's speech for colleagues. "What I understood, and it was a mistake," she explained, "was that [the IRS victory] was going to cascade in other countries, and particularly in Europe. I thought that this was going to be an opening for us in France, and it would change politically in France ... which it didn't." She added, "France doesn't like to be dictated [about] what they need to do. I remember some colleagues also expecting that we were going to be able to pay for services and get them deducted [in our income tax returns]." Another Scientologist invoked the language of war to describe Scientology's past and present in France: "It is [a] kind of war. It's a silent war, but it is a war. . . . If this would happen one hundred years ago, they would shoot us." A Scientologist lawyer in my sample told me that "the main challenge is the full recognition of the Church as a religious body. It's not the case right now, but we will be [recognized] in the future." He noted that many countries in Europe are "turning more favorable to the Church [of Scientology]," in light of legal victories in Spain, Belgium, and the United Kingdom, among others (see e.g., Siuberski, 2016; Arjona & Carrión, 2020; Roux, 2021a), and added that "France could be the last bad student in school" as its neighbors adopt more progressive and inclusive laws for religious minorities.[12]

When I asked interviewees whether they had directly experienced discrimination, persecution, or prejudice in France as a result of their membership in the Church of Scientology, many of the Scientologists in my sample shared personal stories that serve as a reminder of how anticultism can be expressed in cultural and everyday as well as legal and institutional terms. Numerous others knew of others – friends, family, and colleagues – who had been affected by discrimination and anti-*secte* sentiments in the country.

In some cases, interviewees reported instances of violence and threats of violence against Scientologists, churches, and even schools. In fact,

---

[12] Quotations in this section are once again drawn from interviews with French Scientologists in Paris carried out in January 2023.

approximately two weeks before I arrived in France to conduct my first round of interviews in January 2023, one of the Scientology churches in Paris, along with a Scientology center in Copenhagen, was forced to respond to a bomb threat. I interviewed the Scientology staff member who oversaw security at the time. "We checked our emails and we had an email for the Paris Org [church] saying that a guy had planted bombs in plastic bags in the org," she recounted. "I called the cops ... they immediately sent a squad of people." Scientologists on site were evacuated, bomb sniffing dogs were dispatched as a precaution, and ultimately no explosives were found. "This is disrupting all of the org operations," she told me in frustration. "It's a whole thing to bring in the police and the dogs," she went on.

In another incident, which took place just a few months earlier, in late 2022, this same staff member recounted, two men entered the welcome area of the Paris church and approached the receptionist. "One turned and gave a gun to the other one," who loaded it, pointed the pistol at the Scientologist, and pretended to shoot, mimicking the popping sound of a discharged firearm. They were "looking at him in a very evil way. This is threatening. They didn't do anything, then they left, but who knows. They could have." There is a long history of violence and threats of violence against Scientology churches in France. Indeed, the exterior of the Paris Celebrity Centre branch was bombed in April 1984, leaving one Scientologist staff member injured and permanently disabled (*Le Monde,* 1984). One interviewee in my sample was present on the day of this attack. "I'm getting audited and all of a sudden a bomb explodes," he recalled. "A young staff man who was coming out of the door," he went on, was wounded in the face. In March 1997, a bomb, which turned out to be fake, was planted at another Scientology church in Angers (*Courrier de l'Ouest,* 1997). The suspect, who wished to call attention to the "dangers" of *sectes,* was in possession of anti-Scientology literature, as discovered during a police search of his home. He later admitted that he had been heavily influenced by anticult associations and apologized.

Bombings and bomb threats have also been directed against French schools that make use of Hubbard's educational philosophy and methods. In 1984 alone, a Paris music school (*l'Ecole du rythme*) founded by a Scientologist received ten bomb threats by telephone, leading to evacuations and police investigations. This school was also robbed on two occasions, both soon after the airing of anti-Scientology media stories. Perhaps the most prominent educational institution in Paris to make use of Hubbard's Study Technology was the now defunct School of the Awakening, which was bombed on two occasions in the late 1980s (1988 and 1989) and received an additional bomb threat in 1996. I interviewed and informally met several former students of this school. One of them, a second-generation Scientologist, was at the school as a young child at the time of the 1989 bombing. "I remember one time in the school somebody put a bomb that did explode," he remembered. "Actually, my mom was one of the teachers," he continued. "I don't remember hearing a boom, but I remember coming to that place and seeing the thing all blown up and dirty. ... I was like, what the hell? ... At that time, I was a kid. I didn't realize what it meant. I just remember that there was a bomb." Fortunately, no injuries were reported. The bomb threat received in early December 1996 at the School of the Awakening came in the form of an anonymous phone call message: "Your cult will explode in 15 minutes." Students and teachers were evacuated, a bomb squad investigated, and nothing of danger was discovered. The following year, in October 1997, following years of harassment, violence, threats, complaints from some non-Scientology parents about the curriculum, and alleged building code violations – which Scientologists view as a pretext for discrimination – the school was forced to shut down. Students transferred to other schools, and teachers and staff found themselves unemployed.

Some scholars, such as Susan J. Palmer and Stuart A. Wright (2016, 2018), have researched state raids on religious minorities, including those that targeted Scientologists and Scientology organizations in France. One Scientologist in my sample, who works in public and legal affairs for the church, described what she observed in the course of two police raids, both in 2001, at the Church of Scientology Celebrity Centre Paris and Church of Scientology of Paris. With the exception of three colleagues who waited in the cafeteria until the situation cleared, Scientologists were ordered by police to leave the properties and wait outside as the authorities searched the premises and made copies of confidential church files. As a result, she "was alone in the church, going around the church with about ten cops with guns on their jeans." The heavy police presence, she emphasized, was utterly unnecessary and excessive, designed to intimidate Scientologists. In the end, it turned out that the raid was triggered by the mere complaint of a former member who wanted a refund for services. "I had the impression I was in the movie *The Godfather*," as she described the chaotic and overwhelming scene. "You don't need to come with ten guys with a gun. I will answer your questions, except if it's not OK," she explained, "then I'll say, I'm sorry, sir. I am not allowed to answer your questions because you didn't show me the paper saying you can come and do a search. ... I was like, oh, my God. What do they think? That we are criminals and very dangerous people?"

Later in 2001, this same Scientologist, who also served on the board of directors of the Paris church, was arrested and detained by police for thirty-six hours, eventually released and not charged with any crime. Once again, the arrest came after complaints were filed by former members to the police. She insisted on not being handcuffed, which, to her relief, was accommodated. Waiting indefinitely at the police station jail, "I was like, my God, what am I going to do now to get out of here?" She told me, "I was very afraid. . . . I was alone," and was concerned about the possibility of transferring to another jail facility before seeing a judge. "I had heard awful things about it. . . . I was like, 'No, I cannot go there. I'm going to die.'" She remained in the same facility, however, sitting on a wooden bench in a room surrounded by glass, except when moved for interrogations. "They interrogated me nearly the whole day with a sandwich at noon. That's it. Then they put me back in jail at six o'clock at night." She continued, "I spent the whole night in prison," and the following morning a police officer "started to interrogate me again." Finally, she was allowed to leave, and made her way back home on the subway. Describing the ordeal to me more than twenty years later was clearly difficult and emotional. "Now that I am telling it to you again," she admitted with tears in her eyes, "it's like, wow, [what] I went through." "The only way out is the way through," she went on, in reference to an idea found in Hubbard's *Dianetics: The Modern Science of Mental Health* about the need to address and resolve traumatic memories (engrams) head on.[13] "That's how we function. Now that I'm telling you the story again, though, I'm like, oh my God. It's true. It was completely crazy."

Other Scientologists, too, recounted how they had been arrested, and many more knew of church members who had been detained and held in jail for days, and in some cases months, before they were released with no charges filed. I spoke with a lawyer who is also a member of the Church of Scientology and has worked on a variety of religious freedom court cases, both on behalf of Scientology associations and other religious minorities, such as Sikh and Buddhist organizations. He shared the example of a Paris-based Scientologist working in church public affairs who "was put in jail in a case in the south of France in Lyon," after the anticult organization UNADFI merely complained that she was "irresponsible." "The judge put her in jail for three weeks," he told me. "Then, fortunately, a lawyer, not me, succeeded to get her out of the jail, and then she was acquitted. . . . And nothing was against her," he continued, in reference to the absence of charges, "but she went to jail for three weeks . . . it was terrible for her."

Aside from incidents of violence, threats of violence, raids, arrests, and detentions (Figure 4), the most common form of prejudice or persecution described by French Scientologists in my sample concerned workplace

---

[13] For instance, Hubbard wrote in *Dianetics: The Modern Science of Mental Health*: "If he [the preclear] is in the middle of an engram, the only way out of it is *through* it" (2007, p. 477). For more on the history and evolution of Dianetics and Scientology, see Miklovicz (2023).

Figure 4 Scientologists at the Eiffel Tower, protesting the imprisonment of Scientologists by Judge Georges Fenech in a case in Lyon, July 1990. Among those imprisoned was Danièle Gounord, then church spokesperson, who was later acquitted. The sign on the right, in English, reads in part: "They are in prison for their crime of being Scientologists." Courtesy of Éric Roux.

discrimination. One Scientologist spoke about her career as a public school primary (elementary) teacher. In the early 2000s, while teaching at a new school in Paris, a parent recognized her after a protest against a Scientology-affiliated exhibition that resulted in television coverage and a newspaper article that identified her as a Scientologist. The administrator at the school reacted by removing her from a teaching position. "I asked him why," she explained. "He said I created trouble. I said, 'I didn't create trouble. I want to do my work, my job as teacher'. . . . They just said, 'Don't come back, stop, we don't need you as a teacher anymore.'" She managed to stay at the school a few days longer but was soon transferred to a clerical position, out of direct contact with students. Eventually, she managed to transfer to a new school district, also in Paris, and immediately announced to colleagues that she was a Scientologist, as a way to head off any more potential discrimination. This strategy was successful, and she was left alone. This member later left teaching to pursue other employment and now volunteers full time for the church's public relations office.

Several others described how anti-Scientology discrimination and prejudice led to loss of employment in ways that were very often devastating personally as well as financially. In one case, a senior executive in the automotive industry, with years of experience working at companies such as Volkswagen, Renault, and Rover, was dismissed, without cause, following a workplace training event that featured a colleague and fellow Scientologist. During the one-day training session, the organizer mentioned WISE (the World Institute of Scientology Enterprises), a membership body of businesses that uses Hubbard's Administrative Technology (WISE, 2022), and "that he was inspired by Ron Hubbard." About a month later, the executive was called into a meeting and told that he was being let go, ostensibly due to corporate restructuring. He insisted on an explanation, to no avail: "What do you mean? You can't fire me. You have to explain. You have to tell me what happened." In a subsequent meeting, another executive, pressed on the matter, admitted that membership in Scientology led to the layoff. The whole experience "was a shock," he confessed, and caused him to consider moving away from France to another country more friendly to the Church of Scientology. "I think I would have gone, left, and tried a new life elsewhere. Go for the easy, secure, safe position. Take my wife, my child, and go. Maybe I should have moved to America, abroad, but no," he reflected. "I had listened to this song, 'We Stand Tall,' that impressed me, and I applied that. Okay, I'll stand tall. . . . Here I am, and I'm going to do something useful."[14]

In another example, a well-known virtuoso pianist and teacher, Cyprien Katsaris, a longtime Scientologist, spoke about difficulties booking concerts in France and Germany due to his church membership and misinformation about Scientology and Scientologists found online. "It is true that some concert organizers would not invite me because of that, because of the so-called bad image of Scientology in France and Germany," he explained. "The truth of the matter, to be honest with you. . . . I never expected in December '76, when I started, that 45 years later we would still be in this shitty situation. . . . There are many, many, many lies on the Internet."

Other Scientologists were subject to discrimination in the workplace but managed to overcome in ways that did not ultimately lead to loss of employment. One Scientologist, for instance, described working for Panda, the well-known software and security company, which in 2001 was accused in the French media of being a front group for Scientology's alleged infiltration of businesses and governmental databases – all because the founder, Mikel Urizarbarrena, was a Scientologist from Spain. The "Panda Software Scandal," as Susan Palmer has described it, "illustrates France's fear of Scientology as an *American* force of infiltration" (2011, p. 68). In addition to

---

[14] "We Stand Tall" refers to a song, and a music video promoting it, that was released by the Church of Scientology in 1990 (Internet Archive, 1990).

baseless concerns that the use of Panda software programs in France would lead to surveillance and disclosure of confidential information from businesses and state agencies, it was alleged in the media at the time that "money generated by Panda went straight into the coffers of the World Institute of Scientology Enterprises (WISE) in the United States" (Palmer, 2011, p. 68). The bad press caused Panda's sales to crash, and many clients abandoned the software. Employees, some of whom were Scientologists, were targeted along with the product itself. One former employee, a Scientologist, recalled an email sent out to the whole company, as well as its entire client list, presumably from a non-Scientologist employee and critic, warning that it was founded by a Scientologist as part of an effort to "destabilize the company." As a result, "[we] had to see every client one by one to show them that this was not true." Many clients did leave around that time, this Scientologist explained, but Panda survived the loss of revenue and public relations onslaught that threatened its destruction, especially in France.

In still other cases, prejudice, harassment, or discrimination in the workplace was more subtle or covert in nature or else represented an isolated instance that was resolved through open communication. Some members chose to conceal their affiliation with the church for fear of retribution. One Scientologist, a second-generation member who works in the real estate industry, remembered when a coworker discovered some of her mail from the Church of Scientology. "Why didn't you tell me you're in a *secte*?," the coworker asked in dismay. "I told him, 'Are you racist?' He says, 'Oh, no. Never.' I said that the way you talk about my religion, it is hurting me." The colleague immediately apologized, and the issue never came up again. Another Scientologist, a middle-aged woman who has belonged to the church for more than forty years, had not directly experienced problems in the workplace due to her church membership. Fearful that coworkers or managers might retaliate or use Scientology as an excuse to deny promotions and other benefits, she was diligent never to bring up her religion in the first place. "I don't feel I'm free to say I'm a Scientologist even now," she confessed. "Not because people could just not like me, but it could cost me my job. It could cost me my flat. It can cost you, because of the bad things said [about] Scientology and Scientologists." This member clarified that she had no problem sharing about Scientology with non-Scientologist friends outside of work. However, she would not dare tell her manager that she is a Scientologist, "even if there are anti-discrimination laws," she explained, since "maybe they wouldn't feel that this is real discrimination." She elaborated that a manager might even view firing a Scientologist employee as justifiable, even "deserved." This marginalization and fear of retribution speaks not only to anti-*secte* sentiment but also to the dehumanization of members of new and minority religions, something that another Scientologist interviewee put well: "We are really people, and we are just using Scientology tools to be successful and to help us in our life." Yet another Scientologist described the cultural prejudice in the language of presumed guilt: "In France, if you are right but you are a Scientologist, it's different. . . . Of course, you are 'guilty' of something."

I also encountered instances of Scientologists who had been discriminated against or harassed by members of *other* religious communities, in line, for instance, with Massimo Introvigne's distinction between secular *anti*cult and religious *counter*cult movements and sentiments (1995). In one example, a medical doctor and Scientologist working in the east of France lost patients after a local Catholic priest spoke out against him in sermons. "At that time, in 1984, there was a lot of PR and attacks in the media in France," he explained. "The priest said to all the people in the church," the man went on, "don't go to see this doctor because he [will] recruit you to go to the cult." The doctor visited the priest, after numerous patients left his clinic, but the cleric denied that he had spoken out against the man and refused to speak further on the matter. "I say, okay, but I have some people who were there, so they can make a testimony about this," he recalled, to no avail. Ultimately, "I closed my office there and I came back here in Paris." Cyprien Katsaris, the renowned pianist and member of the church, was born into a Greek Orthodox family and well aware of Christian expressions of prejudice against Scientology. "I found out that some of those priests do not appreciate at all that I am a Scientologist," as he put it. "For them, we are considered to be Satanists. It's a total misunderstanding. Also, the Russian Orthodox ones [can hold this anti-Scientology view]." In yet another case, a woman who is both Jewish and a Scientologist encountered resistance from a Conservative rabbi who initially refused to perform a wedding ceremony as a result of her membership in a so-called *secte*. "I was crying just one week before the wedding and it was a big situation," she remembered. In the end, the couple had three separate ceremonies – a Scientology wedding at the Church of Scientology Celebrity Centre in Paris, a Jewish ceremony with a liberal rabbi, and, finally, a private Conservative Jewish wedding as well. This Conservative rabbi, it turned out, wanted to help but was instructed by his advisory board not to get involved due to complaints received about the couple's Scientology affiliation.

Returning to more secular and institutional expressions of anticultism, particularly as advanced through MIVILUDES, UNADFI, CCMM, and FECRIS, several first-generation Scientologists described instances in which their non-Scientologist parents were fearful due to the efforts of anticult organizations and took action to prevent future participation. In one case, a woman was involved in an attempted deprogramming, a practice that amounts to coercion and even kidnapping (see e.g., Massimo Introvigne's Element on the pseudoscientific subject of brainwashing, 2022a). This is another example of the way in which American-born anticultism influenced the theory and practices of NRM opponents outside the United States. The French Scientologist in question, a decades-long member of the church, first joined staff in the 1980s. This upset her father, who, not knowing what to do, reached out to UNADFI for help. One night, at a family dinner, the daughter was confronted by a guest, who turned out to be a volunteer for a local ADFI chapter. The ADFI volunteer had gone so far as to covertly participate in Scientology services in the past, a fact unknown to the other family members at dinner. The Scientologist daughter, however, immediately recognized the woman, since the ADFI volunteer had completed the Purification Rundown (a sauna-based program delivered in the Church of Scientology) and partnered with one of her friends. "I found later," reflecting on the rather confusing situation, that "she had been sent by ADFI to the church" and in reality was an anticult activist. Once the ADFI volunteer's story began to unravel at the dinner table, she lashed out and challenged the neophyte Scientologist, pressing, for instance, on details of church finances. As a relatively new Scientologist, she was not well versed on the intricacies of accounting practices, she admitted, "but I knew very well how it was going with my little [Scientology] association. There were four of us. I knew exactly what was going on with the money." After a heated exchange, the Scientologist agreed to meet with the woman at a later date and continue the conversation, once again at her father's house. "We made an appointment for the next Saturday, 10:00 AM at home," she explained. At this next meeting, she noticed that her father, stepmother, and sister, who had all been in the house, left one by one. "I was alone at home," and finally the volunteer rang the doorbell. "It was just after that I realized that I had been set up by the association with the agreement of my father," she said. This Scientologist opened the door but refused to meet with the ADFI volunteer, who eventually left. Unfortunately, she continued, "that was not the end of the situation." The turn of events and broken trust led to a poor relationship with the father who had arranged the intervention and deprogramming session. The experience showed her firsthand the power and prejudice of anti-*secte* groups in French society.

In France, as in the United States and elsewhere during the "Cult Wars" of the 1970s through 1990s, nonmember parents voiced concerns about children who had joined new and minority religious groups. But today, as the Church of Scientology and other groups have persisted, matured, and expanded on the international religious landscape, there are now multiple generations of members. Several interviewees in Paris recounted instances in which their own children (usually second-generation, but in some cases third-generation,

Scientologists) had suffered discrimination and harassment, especially in school and extracurricular settings. As in earlier decades, this reflects, perhaps, the concern among critics of "cults" that children in such groups may be coerced or manipulated by their parents or church leaders, while ignoring the sociological truth that multiple generations of children are raised within *both* mainstream and alternative religious groups around the world. Recent years have witnessed a rise in academic research on children in new and minority religious groups (see e.g., van Eck Duymaer van Twist, 2015; Frisk, Nilsson, and Åkerbäck, 2018; Nilsson, 2024), including the experience of second-generation Scientologists and others, for instance in Sweden (Åkerbäck, 2018a, 2018b), although much more qualitative and quantitative research ought to be carried out. I did not interview minor children (i.e., under 18 years of age) of French Scientologists in preparation for this work, but the narratives reported by parents reveal qualitative insights into some of the cultural challenges faced by second- and third-generation Scientologists in France. In addition, I interviewed several adult second-generation members who reflected on their own childhoods growing up in the church.

In one such case, a second-generation adult member confessed that it was "not easy" growing up as a French Scientologist, since it was not considered "cool" or fashionable. Another second-generation adult shared that she was bullied and harassed because of her parents' church membership: "When I was 14, I had friends who attacked Scientology a lot." One attributed this prejudice to misinformation – "false data" in Scientology lingo – and unsupportive friends. Another gave insight into the lived realities of second-generation members who study at the church, which requires a great deal of reading materials and listening to Hubbard lectures, with the assistance of transcripts, in line with an emphasis on the importance of defining misunderstood words and concepts as part of the Study Technology. "I'm the generation on YouTube. I like to watch YouTube. I don't like so much to read," she admitted. Although raised in the church, it was not until adulthood that she actively began to seek out Dianetics and Scientology publications, a development that was not forced by her parents, she pointed out. This Scientologist eventually took a course at the church and finally finished reading Hubbard's *Dianetics* (1950) but "was really slow" and "needed almost ten months." However, she benefited greatly from studying Hubbard's nonfiction work, which is counted as scripture of the Church of Scientology – those were her "first big wins" – and led to more courses and advancement on the soteriological Bridge to Total Freedom.

This Scientologist's point that second-generation members freely choose to participate and are not coerced by parents was echoed in other interviews. Moreover, it is reflected in Hubbard's teachings on the importance of freedom of choice and self-determination: "What is true for you is what you have observed *yourself*. And when you lose that, you have lost everything. ... Nothing in Scientology is true for you unless you have observed it and it is true according to your observation" (Church of Scientology International, 2024). One second-generation adult, speaking about a young son, put it as follows: "I am raising him with Scientology data. I like when he comes in the church and for the events, and he is with the other children also." But in the end, she continued, "he will do what he wants. ...I hope he will become a Scientologist. ... We do not force people to be there. For me, I was never forced to be there. I myself said to my mother, 'I want to do a course.'" Another second-generation adult shared much the same experience and sentiment toward her own children. In that case, parents enrolled her in church courses on communication and study, but she continued on her own accord since she enjoyed them and wanted to learn more. "They never pushed me to stay in Scientology."

Many of these same second-generation adult Scientologists shared that their own children have been on the receiving end of anti-*secte* prejudice and discrimination as well. In one example, I learned about the son of Scientologists who had been expelled from a private kindergarten program. "He was just kicked out ... because his parents were Scientologists," I was told by the mother. "This is pure, pure discrimination." This Scientologist attributed the incident to "propaganda against Scientology. That's why finally this kid was kicked out of kindergarten. It's the responsibility of the state," she claimed, in reference to MIVILUDES and associated organizations that receive state funding and promote anti-*secte* messaging in society. In another instance, a nine-year-old stepdaughter was kicked out of a secular scouting organization in the 1990s after she had a conversation with friends about the uses of Study Technology (the girl attended a school that made use of Hubbard's educational philosophy). "We received a phone call from the director of this group," the stepfather explained, "and they said, 'We cannot accept your daughter.' We say, 'Why?'. ... 'It's because you are Scientologists. We cannot accept your daughter.'" He went on, in obvious exasperation, "This is the climate in France. It has a lot of effect on our daughter, by the way. Because after that, she was scared. ... For a long time, she has been scared of being a [daughter] of Scientologists."

In other cases, as reported by their parents, second-generation children of Scientologists were subject to lessons in school about the dangers of *sectes*, including the Church of Scientology. One Scientologist offered an example in which his daughter heard a guest speaker at school denigrate Scientology. "My daughter was actually upset in the class," the father told me, and she even confronted the speaker in front of the teacher and her classmates. "She was like,

'What the hell? You're talking about what my parents are doing. They're doing great in life. They're doing great with me,'" as the father described his daughter's response. "She didn't know how to react. After, she told us she was about to blow, and her friends also knew she was in Scientology." Soon after, he and his wife telephoned the director of the school, complained, and there have so far been no other problems. In another case, a public school teacher gave a lecture on *sectes* and singled out Scientology, leading to pushback, not only from two Scientologist parents who heard about the incident but also from Muslim parents at the same school who sympathized and spoke out to the director in protest and solidarity.

Other Scientologist parents shared how their membership in the church has negatively affected relationships with non-Scientologist parents, sometimes in turn impacting relationships among friends and their children. One interviewee, for instance, spoke about her son, who was very good friends with a boy raised outside the church. The families had known each other for many years and the two boys regularly played sports together, at one point training several hours each day. "We were very close to his parents. Very close," she recalled. "They were coming home. We'd spent New Year's Eve together. . . . I had given my key of the apartment to her son, because he was training every day, just five minutes from us, and he needed to come back and have lunch. . . . One day," though, she explained, "my son told his friend that he was a Scientologist and his friend told the mother." The non-Scientologist mother's reaction was swift and filled with anger: "The mother called us, yelling, and hung up . . . she cut the comm[unication] between the two boys, and he never saw his friend again." Her son later joined the Sea Organization – the Church of Scientology's senior leadership organization and in effect its priesthood (Arjona, 2017) – and, after a couple years, ran into his old childhood friend on a visit to family in Paris. The two caught up and were friendly, the Scientologist mother remembered, but she was upset simply recalling the severed relationships. This, ironically, amounted to a form of "disconnection" in Scientology terminology, but in this case was initiated by a non-Scientologist in response to anti-Scientology prejudice.

Scientologists described other forms of discrimination and prejudice in society. One was discrimination in the banking industry – namely the closure of accounts due to membership in the church. "I remember someone who had a bank account . . . and the bank could say, we closed your account just because you're a Scientologist," one interviewee reported. "Now, it's not so much like this," he clarified, in evidence of some improving attitudes. Still, the larger point was obvious: being a Scientologist in France comes with risks – socially, legally, and financially. However, the Scientologists I met displayed tremendous determination and resilience. For them, the rewards of church membership, personally and collectively, evidently outweighed the risks.

(For readers interested in Scientology's extensive legal history in France, which falls largely outside the scope of this Element, they are referred to English and French sources for legal, scholarly, journalistic, and governmental perspectives. See e.g., Beckford, 1981, 2004; Introvigne, 1995; Introvigne & Melton, 1996; Erhel & de La Baume, 1997; Smith, 2000; Campos, 2001; Hervieu-Léger, 2001a, 2001b; Kent, 2001; Richardson & Introvigne, 2001; Ternisien, 2001; Palmer, 2002, 2008, 2009; Duvert, 2004; Luca, 2004; Richardson, 2009; Machi, 2013; Ollion, 2013; Wright & Palmer, 2016; Carobene, 2017; Pansier, 2018; Garay, 2019; Rigal-Cellard, 2019; Introvigne & Rigal-Cellard, 2022; Koussens, 2023; Church of Scientology International, 2023b. Readers are also referred to the timeline in the Appendix to this Element for a listing of many dates relevant to Scientology legal history and discrimination.)

As of early 2024, there were six Scientology churches and five Scientology missions in France, the largest of which are found in Paris: the Church of Scientology of Paris (7 rue Jules César) and the Church of Scientology Celebrity Centre (69 rue Legendre). However, April 2024 witnessed the consolidation of these two Parisian organizations as they relocated to a new 93,000-square-foot Ideal Organization building as the Church of Scientology and Celebrity Centre of Greater Paris, in the suburb of Saint-Denis (Figure 5).

Figure 5 Church of Scientology and Celebrity Centre of Greater Paris, Saint-Denis, France. Grand opening on April 6, 2024. Church of Scientology International.

Scientology's ecclesiastical leader David Miscavige announced its imminent grand opening at the 39th annual meeting of the International Association of Scientologists (IAS) held in East Grinstead, England, in November 2023 (Church of Scientology International, 2023c). The French Scientologists I met eagerly anticipated the opening of their Ideal Org in Saint-Denis, while remaining aware of the challenges ahead and the resurgence of anticultism represented by the likes of MIVILUDES, UNADFI, CCMM, and FECRIS.

Scientologists in Paris offered their perspectives on what the new Ideal Org Church of Scientology in Saint-Denis means to them personally, institutionally, and for the future of the Scientology religion in France. "Finally," one said,

> We will have a church where we can practice our religion exactly as it was intended by LRH [L. Ron Hubbard], in a church that contains every space that is necessary for a full delivery of our religious services, with no shortage of space and also the needed room for accepting people who might be interested in our humanitarian programs.

The Ideal Org project, then, from a Scientological point of view, represents the realization of Hubbard's ecclesiastical and theological intentions (Hubbard, 1970; Church of Scientology International, 2023a), in line, for instance, with Mikael Rothstein's research on Scientology architecture and the Weberian routinization of charisma (2014). "The Ideal Org is not just the building, of course," explained one Scientologist. "It's the people, and there are the people, they're going to be in a place that is ideal. The CC [Celebrity Centre] and the [Paris] Org, they're great orgs, but they're very small, and so it's going to be huge, and it's going to be perfect and ideal." The new church in Saint-Denis, in turn, is seen by members as an essential step in the acceptance and flourishing of Scientology in France for those who want it; that is to say, as part of its missiological as well as ecclesiastical goals. With the new church, one Scientologist told me: "[Scientology] will be real for people. ... I'm telling you, in France, we are not real. We need this Ideal Org to be real. ... we are too small now. For people, the new generation, they're just on Instagram, TikTok.... They need big, big things to be real. Otherwise, they're just looking at the screen and the real world is not real for them." Another Scientologist put the new church project in the larger context of European legal recognitions. "We need to take every person one by one and show them what we do, what we do in the world, so that people could realize that actually Scientology is recognized as a religion in Spain, in Italy, in [the] UK, and all over and we are in the middle of France." Despite Scientologists' enthusiasm and support of their church and its mission, I also detected among interviewees a deep respect for freedom of religion and belief, and an acknowledgment that conversion to Scientology is not necessarily the immediate goal, in recognition of cultural and religious diversity and freedom of choice, especially in a relatively secular country such as France. "We don't need people to become Scientologists," one member explained. "We just want to provide our tools and our help so they can be successful. Then if they want to become Scientologists, good. If they don't, good. Your choice."

3 Reflections on the Future of New and Minority Religions in France

Dianetics and Scientology have been part of France's intellectual and religious landscape since the 1950s, alongside numerous other new or alternative religious, spiritual, and philosophical communities. Today, despite institutional growth, the Church of Scientology, alongside religious minorities at large in France, continues to face social and legal obstacles. With renewed vigor and fresh funding, MIVILUDES has emerged from the COVID-19 pandemic, and NRMs such as Scientology and Jehovah's Witnesses find themselves targeted alongside alternative medical providers. A resurgence of anticultism highlights contemporary concerns with public health, as well as "cultic" abuse, all in the name of *laïcité* and the perceived public good for the body politic.

It seems to me, though, that a body such as MIVILUDES is quite likely as unnecessary as it is unconstitutional within France. The group is arguably not needed, first of all, because laws already exist, as they do in most countries, to investigate and prosecute instances of abuse, meaning that there is no special or additional need for attention to so-called *sectes* as a categorically separate or unique instance of abuse if and when it occurs. Meanwhile, MIVILUDES, even more fundamentally, appears to be unconstitutional within France because it violates commitments to freedom of belief *and* expressions of those beliefs within communities of like-minded individuals or associations. The continued existence of MIVILUDES, from my perspective as an NRM researcher, is a grave concern for freedom of religion advocates in Europe and internationally, as well as researchers concerned about prejudice against new and minority religious communities. In addition, the anti-*secte* discrimination at the heart of its mission stands in violation to the Universal Declaration of Human Rights (1948, Article 18), which in December 2023 celebrated its 75th anniversary: "Everyone has the right to freedom of thought, conscience and religion; this right includes freedom to change his religion or belief, and freedom, either alone or in community with others and in public or private, to manifest his religion or belief in teaching, practice, worship and observance." It also appears to stand in violation to the similarly phrased Article 9 of the European Convention on Human Rights, except in that case one discovers a rather subjective clause: "Freedom to manifest one's religion or beliefs shall be subject only to such limitations as are prescribed by law and are necessary in a democratic society in the interests of public safety, for the protection of public order, health or morals, or for the protection of the rights and freedoms of others" (Council of Europe, 2020). After all, what objective criteria might exist – ones that are free from bias and prejudice about desirable versus undesirable religious and spiritual groups – in determining when legal "limitations" are indeed "necessary" or, in fact, become excessive, intrusive, discriminatory, and indeed illegal? In France, more to the point, how is it possible to balance respect for *individual* freedom of religion or belief (FORB), as enshrined in the French constitution (Article 1), with competing and often contradictory understandings of the nature and role of *laïcité* in modern French society? If, as sociologist Véronique Altglas has argued, "*laïcité* is as *laïcité* does" (2010), paradoxically and even hypocritically, within a framework of gradations, then what does this imply about the role of the state to, if and when necessary, counteract anti-*secte* activism as exemplified by MIVILUDES or other threats to religious liberty? And what can and should be done when, in the case of MIVILUDES, it is, in effect, the *state* itself that lies at the heart of the problem from the perspective of FORB advocates? What are possible paths forward in light of a governmental "schizophrenia," as the Scientologist lawyer in my sample framed it, in which the *Bureau des Cultes* apparently wants little, if anything, to do with hardline anti-*secte* expressions of state secularism?

These questions are difficult to answer and largely depend on one's cultural background and views on how religious diversity ought to be expressed within a particular milieu. However, it seems altogether likely that MIVILUDES will be forced to reform itself or possibly even dissolve, which would, in turn, siphon funding to dependent and associated anticult organizations such as UNADFI and CCMM. In fact, a legal effort is underway in France in an attempt to dissolve FECRIS (Fautré, 2023). If French anticultism has turned its attention in recent years, as Altglas has described and I would agree, to "non-religious domains of social life as a major factor in explaining the recent revitalization of the cult controversy" (2010, p. 501), then this suggests a gradual shift in the mission of MIVILUDES that might render it irrelevant for yet another reason: it has implicitly given up, for the most part, on its monitoring of *sectes* and must justify its continued existence by other means, especially in the domain of alternative medicine. On the one hand, this new direction might be interpreted as a kind of Fabian victory for opponents of *sectes* in France, whose long-term attrition strategy has indeed oppressed many new and alternative religious groups out of existence or even further into the margins of society. On the other hand, though, it may even be interpreted as a quasi-cultural victory for the so-called cults that have persisted in the face of persecution, especially the Jehovah's Witnesses and Scientologists, whose resilience seems to have won the day, even if cultural and legal challenges remain for them and other groups. These include the anthroposophical movement, Plymouth Brethren, Wiccan groups, Soka Gakkai, Sahaja Yoga, Brahma Kumaris, and Church of Almighty God as well as numerous Catholic and Evangelical groups, such as the Community of the Beatitudes, Missionary Family of Notre-Dame, ACER (*Assemblée Chrétienne pour l'Évangélisation et le Réveil*, Christian Assembly for Evangelization and Revival), the Universal Church of the Kingdom of God, Charisma Church, Impact Centre Chrétien, and Alliance of Nations for Jesus Christ. One major recent challenge is an effort to strengthen the 2001 About-Picard Law regarding "psychological subjection" (i.e., notions of brainwashing, mind control, and coercion) (Barker, 2024). The proposed legislation – which was passed in April 2024 but as of this writing was contested by French parliamentarians and is in the hands of the Constitutional Council (*Conseil Constitutionnel*) – had prompted the chairman of the US Commission on International Religious Freedom (USCIRF), Abraham Cooper, to condemn it on the grounds that it would "allow govt orgs [government organizations] known to target religious minority groups like Jehovah's Witnesses & Scientologists to participate in cult-related criminal proceedings" (Introvigne, 2023f). In July 2023, a USCIRF report singled out FECRIS and MIVILUDES in more explicit terms, noting for instance that the latter "has partnered with government agencies, religious organizations, and civil society to inform them about so-called 'cults' and has generated largely positive reactions from French media outlets, which has in turn negatively impacted societal respect for those associated with religious organizations that MIVILUDES labels as sects or cults" (Blum, 2023).

Certainly in the case of the Church of Scientology, persistence and resilience in the face of legal, governmental, and media challenges is at the heart of Scientological theology and culture. A church spokeswoman in the United States once explained that Scientology is "not a turn-the-other-cheek type of religion" (Westbrook, 2019, p. 115), and that is undoubtedly true in light of the church's proactive public relations and legal strategies. This resilient attitude of Scientologists is something that is in fact baked into, as it were, Scientology teachings. As far back as Hubbard's *Dianetics: The Modern Science of Mental Health*, first published in 1950, this mindset is discernible in what are referred to there as "black panther" mechanisms with respect to the hypothetical situation of responding to a threatening panther. Five responses are offered: "*attack, flee, avoid, neglect* or *succumb*" (2007, p. 181). Whether one is handling engrams (traumatic memories) or public relations and legal challenges, attack or counterattack, as the case may be, is the preferable and productive course of action, one that is poised to actively resolve the situation and, more than that, ensure long-term survival and success, both individually and collectively. This adaptive and resilient attitude also explains the longevity and legal victories of French Jehovah's Witnesses, who have likewise neither fled nor succumbed to pressures that might have otherwise driven them out of the country (see e.g., Introvigne, 2021). In the case of new and minority religious groups, the present-day "panther" seems to come in the form of threats posed by MIVILUDES, FECRIS, and anticult allies.

Finally, viewing the problem of anticultism from the perspective of NRM studies, it should be emphasized that the terms in questions are of course contested. After all, one person's *secte* or cult is another person's religion. As J. Gordon Melton has put it, "Cults are groups you don't like" (Westbrook, 2014), a subjectivity that plays out among individuals but also among groups and even nation–states, with the word cult employed within and outside of traditional religious contexts as well (see e.g., Roux, 2023a, 2023b, 2023c). Indeed, as far as I can tell, many French citizens are ambivalent about the "problem" of *sectes* and this attitude came up several times in my interviews. With respect to Scientology, one interviewee acknowledged the reputational damage caused by the media while noting that most French citizens know very little, if anything, beyond stereotypes.[15] "It's a difficult question. I think that people do not know anything about Scientology," according to this Scientologist. She continued: "Most people in the street, they don't know what it is. Maybe they have heard it's a cult. ... Then they will just repeat what they maybe read or heard, or what they understood. Very often also they will say, 'Oh, Tom Cruise.'" The implication that relatively few French citizens have firsthand experiences, friendships, or family that would bring them into contact with members of new, alternative, and minority communities suggests that another antidote to French anticultism is far simpler than dissolving MIVILUDES or protesting anti-*secte* legislation. That is, getting to know one's neighbors, colleagues, friends, and fellow citizens and respecting their beliefs, practices, and cultures on their own terms. This means putting into practice the ideals of *liberté*, *égalité*, and, perhaps especially, *fraternité*.

---

[15] In 2018, for instance, IFOP, an opinion polling company in France, surveyed 1,000 French adults on their views of religion, secularism, and Scientology and, among other findings, revealed that 79 percent agreed that religion should be a private matter and religious authorities should not take a public position on major social issues ("La religion relève de la vie privée et les autorités religieuses ne devraient pas prendre position publiquement sur"). In addition, 38 percent of respondents agreed that the Church of Scientology has been subject to exaggerated or caricatured criticism in France ("Fait l'objet de critiques caricaturales") (IFOP, 2018).

Appendix
Selected Timeline of Anticultism in France, with Special Reference to Scientology History

1901: Law on Associations passed in France.

1905: Law on the Separation of the Churches and the State passed.

1949: Mario Feninger, later a founding figure of Scientology in France, studied general semantics under Alfred Korzybski in the United States. The following year, Feninger was introduced to L. Ron Hubbard's *Dianetics* (1950).

May 9, 1950: Hubbard's *Dianetics: The Modern Science of Mental Health* first published in the USA (Hermitage House, New York).

1954/1955: Mario Feninger meets John M. "Jack" Campbell, an American student of Dianetics. Campbell worked for Hubbard in Paris, delivered a "course" of Scientology (what Campbell referred to as a "Salon de Scientologie") and established a "Scientological liaison" in Paris by the end of 1954.

1956: Campbell is ordained a Scientology Minister and describes himself as "Bishop of Paris" in a letter to Hubbard (March 11). Campbell represents HASI (Hubbard Association of Scientologists International) in France and the official address of the HASI in Paris is Campbell's address.

1956: L. Ron Hubbard visited Paris and was photographed in front of the Arc de Triomphe.

October 26, 1959: *Les Amis de la Scientologie* (The Friends of Scientology) association founded by Feninger and Campbell registered in Paris.

December 27, 1968: Hubbard Association of French Scientologists founded.

March 10, 1971: Scientology center in Paris raided by police for the first time, triggered by an anonymous letter suggesting that the Scientology center had a link with far-left extremists living in the neighborhood.

April 26, 1971: Church of Scientology of France/Hubbard Association of Scientology founded.

November 9, 1971: Scientology mission center of Le Bois D'Oingt (near Lyon) established.

March 21, 1974: Scientology mission center of Versailles established.

September 10, 1974: Scientology mission center of Angers established.

November 29, 1974: Citizens Commission on Human Rights, an antipsychiatric activist group affiliated with the Church of Scientology, established a branch in Paris.

December 12, 1974: Creation of the first ADFI (*Association de défense des familles et de l'individu*, Association for the Defense of Families and the Individual) in Rennes. In 1982, the umbrella group UNADFI (*Union nationale des associations de défense des familles et de l'individu*, National Union of Associations for the Defense of Families and Individuals) was founded to unite ADFI chapters spread across France.

December 22, 1975: French Association of Scientology and the Church of Scientology of France–Cultural Association of Paris founded.

May 22, 1977: Michel de Certeau, a renowned Catholic theologian, writes that he is "fully convinced of the legitimacy of using the term 'religion' for the Church of Scientology, since these texts all express a spiritualism based on an infinite Being, expressed socially through a community life (meetings, ministers, tradition) and an organization of specific behaviors." He "also admired this articulation between ethical concerns, a search for wisdom and technical training."

May 24, 1977: Scientology's drug treatment program Narconon established in France.

May 26, 1977: Scientology mission center of Lyon-Sarcey (La Chana-Sarcey) established.

August 4, 1977: Association for the Study of the New Faith (a Scientology group) founded.

August 10, 1977: New Understanding–Cultural Association of Paris (a Scientology group) founded.

November 2, 1977: Maurice Cordier, a well-known Catholic priest and activist with the French resistance during World War II, writes a testimony in favor of Scientology.

1978: L. Ron Hubbard convicted, *in absentia*, of fraud in France, and sentenced to four years in prison. Three other Scientologists are convicted of fraud in France but acquitted on appeal. L. Ron Hubbard, who had not been in France since the 1950s, was never summoned so could never appeal, but eminent French legal experts, such as Georges Levasseur (1907–2003), wrote that he would have been acquitted along with the others. In 2013, a French Court of Appeal ruled that the conviction was rehabilitated (expunged) and should be considered as never having existed.

January 1979: University course on *sectes* (cults) offered at the University Pierre et Marie Curie (Jussieu) in Paris.

February 1979: Anticult conference held at the Ecole Polytechnique in Paris. The theme is "Cults, disease of the modern world."

September 1, 1979: Official registration of the Celebrity Centre of Paris, Rue de la Tour d'Auvergne.

May 22, 1980: Church of Scientology of Angers founded.

August 7, 1980: Church of Scientology of Saint-Étienne founded.

December 1980: ADFI international meeting held in Paris.

1981: CCMM (*Centre contre les manipulations mentales*, Center against Mind Control) founded by Roger Ikor.

January 1982: Jean Ravail, a senior civil servant, presents a report called "Note on the activities of pseudo-religious associations" to the Minister of the Interior, proposing repressive measures against *sectes*.

Early 1982: Former NRM member who had undergone deprogramming, based on techniques introduced into France by Marie-Christine Cordon, commits suicide on the premises of an ADFI chapter.

March 4, 1982: Church of Scientology of Clermont-Ferrand founded.

March 11, 1982: Church of Scientology of Lyon founded.

March 1982: The magazine "Les Dossiers de l'Histoire" (The History Files) publishes a long article by Dr. Serge Bornstein, a renowned French psychiatrist, which concludes: "L. R. Hubbard has established himself as a major figure of the 20th century, and his religious philosophy ranks among the great spiritual currents of humanity."

1982: UNADFI (*Union Nationale des Associations de Défense des Familles et de l'Individu victimes de Sectes*, National Union of Defense of Families and the Individual victims of cults) founded. UNADFI becomes the umbrella organization for local ADFI chapters in France.

1983: National police raid Scientology center in St. Etienne.

1983: Alain Vivien, a member of the French Parliament from the Socialist party and Freemason, publishes *Les sectes en France*. Vivien was commissioned to produce this by Prime Minister Pierre Mauroy. The work establishes a typology that includes the concept *secte absolue* ("absolute cult"), regarded as the most harmful and dangerous, which is applied to Scientology. In 1998, Vivien became director of MILS (*Mission Interministerielle de Lutte contre les Sectes*, Interministerial Mission to Combat Cults).

1983/84: Two dozen criminal complaints filed against the Church of Scientology by former Scientologists, including Julia Darcondo and Chantal Carrière, who are affiliated with UNADFI. After two decades of investigation, no wrongdoing was found and the charges were dismissed.

1984: Director of the School of Rhythm (*l'Ecole du rythme*), a music school founded by a Scientologist that uses Hubbard's Study Technology educational methods, reports ten bomb threats by telephone. This leads to the evacuation of the school and police investigation. The school was also robbed twice after anti-Scientology media stories.

April 2, 1984: Bomb detonates outside the Church of Scientology Celebrity Centre of Paris. One Scientologist is injured and permanently disabled.

February 1, 1985: The *Conseil d'État* (Council of State, France's highest administrative court) recognizes a Jehovah's Witnesses congregation as an *association cultuelle* (religious association) per the law of 1905. This will be the first of a long series of decisions favorable to the recognition of the Jehovah's Witnesses in France.

1985: Scientology executives François Bonnet and Alain Franck Rosenberg are indicted by Judge Guilbaud and asked to prove the scientific basis of the Purification Rundown. They respond with a complaint against the judge for violating religious freedom. They will not be convicted and the case will eventually be dismissed in 2010.

1985: Scientologist Michel Raoust creates *Comite francais des Scientologues contre la discrimination* (French Committee of Scientologists against Discrimination).

1985: Epileptic woman dies at Scientology-affiliated Narconon Grancey center in the Dijon region. A prefect closes the center, and two staff members are arrested and fined, with the fine reduced on appeal.

Spring 1985: Lesson on *sectes* given in Paris public schools, with Scientology singled out as dangerous and that Scientologists are "devious and abnormal people."

April 1985: Alain Vivien's report on *sectes* released by the official publishing house of the government. The report is criticized by Christian groups (Catholic and Protestant alike) as a threat to freedom of religion in France.

October 1985: *Conseil d'État* decision that Scientology organizations will be subject to corporation taxes as profit-based associations.

October 5, 1985: Scientologist Michel Raoust receives the International Association of Scientologists (IAS) Freedom Medal for his defense of religious freedom in France.

1986: Four criminal complaints filed against *l'Ecole du Rhythme* in Paris. One of the complaints is filed by Solange Jeandroz, who later worked for UNADFI and then created an independent anticult group called *l'Alouette* (the Lark). No convictions will result from these complaints, which will be dismissed.

1987: Police raid Grancey Scientology center.

October 11, 1987: Scientologist and professional race car driver Philippe de Henning receives IAS Freedom Medal. He raced in a Dianetics-themed car, at the *24 hours of Le Mans*, during this period, winning in 1987.

November 12, 1987: Death of Roger Ikor, the founder of the anticult association CCMM. Marie Geneve becomes president of the association, but, behind the scenes, Roger Leray, formerly Grand Master of the masonic lodge Grand Orient de France, and Catholic priest Jean-François Six, are said to be running the association.

Late 1987: William Connett, an opponent of Scientology who was formerly head of an IRS office in California, appointed as an IRS representative in France, with an office in the American embassy.

December 1987: Scientologist Anne Piquereau, a French athlete and two-time national champion in the 100-meter hurdles, subject to discrimination by the Ministry of Sport. She received threats from employees in the ministry, resulting in sponsorship losses.

December 31, 1987: Tax office in Pau issues a decision that donations for courses at the Pau Scientology mission center are tax-deductible.

February 22, 1988: Bomb detonates in the early morning in front of the Scientology-affiliated School of Awakening in Paris, a school that uses Hubbard's Study Technology. No injuries are sustained.

March 24, 1988: Death in Lyon of Patrice Vic, who had completed some introductory Scientology courses. The death is ruled a suicide, which is disputed by Scientologists. While the police dismiss the case after an initial investigation, it is reopened and led by Georges Fenech, a judge who will become a rabid opponent of the Church of Scientology and later the head of MIVILUDES. The suicide leads to a court case against the church and a conviction for fraud and involuntary homicide for fifteen Scientologists. A Court of Appeal will acquit ten of them on July 28, 1997 and state that "the Church of Scientology may claim the title of religion and freely develop its activities, including missionary activities, within the framework of existing laws."

October 4, 1988: The Ladame case, involving the Scientologist who was injured in the bombing of the Church of Scientology Celebrity Centre in Paris, is heard. The social security office in France (URSSAF) claims that full-time staff members of the Church of Scientology in France should be salaried. Later, URSSAF agrees that staff members who hold religious positions (as opposed to, for example, accountants) should not be salaried.

April 25, 1989: Molotov cocktail thrown against the window of the Scientology mission in Nice, resulting in property damage.

July 1989: Book club "France Loisir" ceases distribution of Hubbard's science fiction books (*Battlefield Earth* and the *Mission Earth* series) and offers refunds to members, after a smear campaign against Scientology by UNADFI.

Mid-1989: Large-scale campaign to promote *Dianetics:The Modern Science of Mental Health* in France, assisted by Scientologists and celebrity members such as opera singer Julia Migenes. During this time, representatives from local ADFI offices protested bookstores for selling the book and radio stations that promote church-affiliated public relations campaigns. This causes some booksellers to withdraw *Dianetics* from their stores.

August 25, 1989: Claude Junqua, a former Scientologist (later known as Mona Vasquez), begins a hunger strike in front of the Church of Scientology of Paris. She seeks a refund for Scientology services and, after three days, is taken to a hospital for physical problems. The Church will refund her payments.

October 1, 1989: Another bomb detonates at the School of Awakening.

1990: Six police raids on Scientology centers (May 16: Nice and Marseille; June 26: Lyon; July 4: Paris) leading to the arrest of Scientologists. Twenty-four Scientologists were put in custody for two days in Marseille and Nice, four of whom remained incarcerated for several months. In Lyon, four Scientologists were arrested and incarcerated for several months. In Paris, six were arrested, two of whom remained incarcerated for several months. No trials were ever held, following a twenty-year criminal investigation. In 2010, the Court of Cassation confirmed a 2009 Court of Appeal decision to dismiss the case because no wrongdoing was found.

May 17, 1990: Xavier Delamare, head of the Nice and Marseille Scientology missions, is held by police and questioned for four hours in the early morning (2:30 AM to 6:30 AM). Delamare's leg was broken, and he received no treatment while in police custody for a total of forty-eight hours.

July 1990: Marie-Ange Molina, a Scientology staff member from Nice indicted by a judge, begins a ten-day hunger strike in prison.

August 2, 1990: Police search the Scientology mission in Lyon. Judge Georges Fenech, a vocal critic of the Church of Scientology, is present along with members of the RG (French secret police). Preclear and other administrative files are seized. Scientologists are held by the police. During interrogations, police sometimes read passages out loud from confidential files, which contain private data from auditing/counseling sessions. The raid on the Lyon mission also leads to a temporary ban on Scientologists visiting the mission center and a ban on selling *Dianetics* books.

October 6, 1990: Opera singer Julia Migenes receives IAS Freedom Medal for her support of religious freedom and information campaigns about Dianetics and Scientology in Europe and the United States.

November 5, 1990: Scientologists Xavier Delamare and Marie-Ange Molina, from Nice, are released from prison after five and a half months. They are placed under judicial supervision and reside with their parents.

March 1991: Jean Galéa, a Scientologist and professor at a university in Marseille, discovered dozens of posters at work naming him as a member of the church and a leader of a *secte*.

May 15, 1991: In Reims, a *juge d'instruction* (investigating judge) dismisses a fraud case against the Church of Scientology of Reims, stating that no wrongdoing can be proven.

October 1, 1991: Police raid Scientology center in Paris.

November 7, 1991: Deprogramming of Scientologist and nurse Maria Crapanzano. Dr. Jean-Marie Abgrall, psychiatrist and advocate for deprogramming of French "cult" members, is involved. He advises a colleague, Dr. Robert Guerrini, to carry out a deprogramming even though Abgrall never met or evaluated the individual. Crapanzano is involuntarily placed in the Sainte Marguerite hospital in Marseille and later files a criminal complaint for kidnapping and forcible confinement, resulting in a 1996 conviction for Dr. Guerrini for making false medical statements.

January 13, 1992: Police search the Church of Scientology of Paris and Celebrity Centre in Paris. Twenty-five Scientologists are taken into custody and interrogated. The homes of seven members are searched. Computers at the churches are searched and documents are seized by police from church centers. Fifteen Scientologists are indicted for fraud and other crimes. The case will be dismissed years later in 2010.

April 1992: Scientology-affiliated publication *Éthique et Liberté* (Ethics and Freedom) publishes an article about the deprogramming of Anne-Catherine Bouvier de Cachard, an alleged Scientologist. She undergoes deprogramming with support from family members and UNADFI allies, although she is not a Scientologist and her confinement was used within a family dispute. Anne-Catherine spends a week in a psychiatric hospital and is placed on antipsychotic medication. The woman's sisters sue *Éthique et Liberté* for defamation. The case is ultimately decided in favor of the magazine/church, and the sisters go on to found the anticult organization "Secticide," which speaks out against Scientology and other groups.

April 13, 1992: Eric Dumas de La Roque, a former Scientologist, begins hunger strike outside the Church of Scientology of Paris. He seeks 480,000 francs from the Paris church, although these funds were initially paid to another Scientology entity, the Flag Church, in Clearwater, Florida. The Paris church files two complaints, for extortion and a false accusation. During the hunger strike and protest, a Scientologist is injured and taken to the hospital, while the arm of a Scientologist receptionist is broken. During the hunger strike/protest, a fire is started outside the church and extinguished. The protest receives media attention due to publicity by UNADFI and critics such as Didier Lerouge.

May 1992: Court of Appeal of Douai sentences Dianetics center in Lille with a fine for defaming UNADFI.

August 1992: Jacques Cotta and Pascal Martin publish *Dans le secret des sectes* (In the Secret of Cults) with Editions Flammarion.

October 7, 1992: FIREPHIM (*la Fédération Internationale des Religions et Philosophies Minoritaires*, International Federation of Minority Religions and Philosophies) founded by Rael, leader of the International Raelian Movement.

October 8, 1992: Town Hall of Clichy-la-Garenne issues an order prohibiting the Church of Scientology from selling books or distributing fliers in the commune of Clichy. This is annulled four years later, on March 22, 1996, by an administrative court, which found it in violation of religious freedom.

December 12, 1992: Private UNADFI-sponsored meeting held with anticult lawyers and representatives from the Ministry of the Interior and Ministry of Defense to discuss possible legal and media strategies against French *sectes*, in particular Scientology. One of the attendees, a law student, later described the meeting in affidavits, including goals to attack new religions in the press ("The idea would be to start again with Scientology and especially to continue until Scientology disappeared completely in France").

January 13, 1993: Importation into France of Scientology books prohibited by a directive authored by Jean-Marc Sauve, Director of Public Liberties and Legal Affairs of the Ministry of the Interior.

October 11, 1993: Church of Scientology of Angers receives tax inspection. This comes less than two weeks after the IRS recognized American churches as tax-exempt nonprofit organizations. The inspection in Angers leads to a tax adjustment costing the church 200,000 francs.

1993: Journalist Serge Faubert publishes *Une secte au cœur de la République: Les réseaux français de l'Eglise de scientologie* (A Cult at the Heart of the Republic: The French Networks of the Church of Scientology). Scientology in France is described as a tool for American imperialism.

April 1994: Anti-*secte* organization Secticide founded in Verdun.

June 1994: FECRIS (*Fédération Européenne des Centres de Recherche et d'Information sur le Sectarisme*, European Federation of Centers of Research and Information about Cults and Sects) founded in Paris. It monitors *sectes* ("cults") in France and throughout Europe via affiliated groups. Its headquarters are at the same address as UNADFI, which is listed as a cofounder.

February 1995: American deprogrammer and anticult activist Steven Hassan publishes *Protect Yourself Against Cults*, originally released in English, in France, as *Protégez-vous contre les sectes*. The French version includes a preface by Dr. Jacques Richard, former head of UNADFI and president of FECRIS.

March 1995: CCMM book published by Albin Michel with public funding, *Les Sectes, état d'urgence: Mieux les connaître, mieux s'en défendre en France et dans le monde* (Cults, State of Emergency: Get to Know Them Better, Better Defend Against Them in France and Around the World). Numerous groups are mentioned, with particular attention paid to Scientology.

July 1995: Parliamentary Commission on Sectes in France following the Order of the Solar Temple murders/suicides. This is followed by commissions in 1999 and 2006.

November 30, 1995: Tribunal of Commerce of Paris declares bankruptcy of Scientology churches in France due to unpaid back taxes (totaling 48 million francs). The church counters that it was never required to pay these taxes due to its religious status. Eventually, the Church of Scientology in the United States attempts to pay the balance, but the transfer is deliberately blocked by French authorities. The bankruptcy is canceled after a legal challenge ruled that the transfer and payment should have been allowed. On December 8, 2000, the *Conseil d'État* (Council of State, France's highest administrative court) condemned the French State and awarded 12,000 francs in damages to be paid to the Church. The Council of State, during the proceeding, submitted a question to the Court of Justice of the European Union, which responded that the blocked payment was illegal.

December 1995: The Guyard Report first released in the National Assembly. French and European-wide media attention to *sectes*, in the wake of the Solar Temple murders/suicides, leads to anti-Scientology news coverage and public opinion and prejudice against NRMs and religious minorities in general.

1995: *Coordination des Associations et des Particuliers pour la Liberté de Conscience* (Coordination of Associations and Individuals for Freedom of Conscience, also known as CAP Freedom of Conscience or CAP LC) founded. It later received consultative status with the United Nations.

January 10, 1996: Formal publication of Report of the Parliamentary Commission of Inquiry into Sects. The chairman is Alain Gest and the rapporteur (reporter for the commission) is Jacques Guyard, hence the shorthand Guyard Report or Gest-Guyard Report. The report lists 173 movements, including the Church of Scientology. The list is based on a report from the RG (*Renseignements Généraux*, French intelligence service). The director of the RG at the time, Yves Bertrand, later reflected: "I believe that the American concept is not without merit. We have the right to criticize Scientology or Jehovah's Witnesses, but do we have to turn them into devils? In fact, I believe that equating certain thinking movements with genuine sectarian movements achieves the opposite of what it was intended to do."

January 26, 1996: Mayor of Angers issues prohibition against the sale of *Dianetics* books in the city; the prohibition will later be canceled in court.

February 29, 1996: French government releases circular to the public "relative à la lutte contre les atteintes aux personnes et aux biens commises dans le cadre des mouvements à caractère sectaire" ("relating to the fight against attacks on people and property committed within the framework of movements of a sectarian nature").

March 15, 1996: A group of anarchists vandalizes the Church of Scientology in Lyon with paint and gas. Windows are broken and the Scientologists inside are forced out due to fumes.

May 1996: Interministerial Observatory on Cults created by Prime Minister Alain Juppé. In 1998, it will be replaced by MILS.

May 1996: Psychiatrist Jean-Marie Abgrall publishes *La mécanique des sectes* (The Mechanics of Cults) with Payot.

1996: Massimo Introvigne and J. Gordon Melton's edited volume, *Pour en finir avec les sectes* (To Put an End to Cults), is released in response to the 1996 Guyard Report; this publication includes a chapter on Scientology by British sociologist Bryan R. Wilson.

1996: Religious freedom group *Omnium des Libertés* founded by Joël Labruyère.

November 1996: Fifteen Scientologists are convicted of fraud in connection with the 1988 suicide of Patrice Vic. This includes Jean-Jacques Mazier, sentenced to eighteen months in prison and fined 500,000 francs. Most of the Scientologists are acquitted or received suspended sentences on appeal. The investigating judge was Georges Fenech, a vocal critic of Scientology and a future head of MIVILUDES (*Mission interministérielle de vigilance et de lutte contre les dérives sectaires*, Interministerial Mission of Vigilance and Combat against Cultic Deviance).

December 5, 1996: Bomb threat at the School of Awakening in Paris. An anonymous phone call is received: "Your cult will explode in 15 minutes." Children and staff are evacuated. Police and a bomb squad investigate, but no explosives are found. (Ten years earlier, two bombs exploded at this school.)

December 18, 1996: The Court of Lille issues a judgment stating that the Church of Scientology is exempt from requirements regarding the treatment of personal data, as "churches and religious or philosophical groups" are exempt per the data protection law.

February 10, 1997: Two skinheads attempt to set fire to the Church of Scientology of Clermont-Ferrand. They are arrested and sentenced to three months' imprisonment.

March 7, 1997: Bomb planted at the Church of Scientology in Angers. Police are called and the area is closed off. The bomb turns out to be fake.

A search of the suspect's home by the police uncovers anti-Scientology media materials, and the suspect tells authorities that he wished to call attention to the dangers of cults. The perpetrator is sentenced to eighteen months in prison (with sixteen months suspended). He later admitted that he had acted after reading anti-Scientology reports from anticult associations. He apologized and encouraged others to engage in peaceful dialogue.

June 1997: Janine Tavernier receives Legion of Honor for efforts against *sectes* (cults) in France.

July 10, 1997: Commercial Court of Paris liquidates the Church of Scientology Celebrity Centre of Paris over liability of 1.8 million francs, most of which is disputed debt in a case involving Didier Lerouge.

July 28, 1997: Religious recognition of the Church of Scientology by the Court of Appeal in Lyon: "Scientology is entitled to call itself a religion and to freely develop within the framework of existing laws its activities." This is followed by anti-Scientology coverage in the media and anti-Scientology rhetoric by members of Parliament.

October 17, 1997: School of the Awakening forced to close following years of harassment, bombings, bomb threats, alleged building code violations, and accusations that the head of school misled others about the use of Hubbard's Study Technology in the curriculum. The school is liquidated after a legal decision because it could not pay tax debts per a court plan. (This school had previously received subsidies from the French State, but these were canceled in 1983 due to the school's affiliation with Scientologists and the use of Hubbard's educational philosophy and techniques.)

November 7, 1997: Ministry of the Interior issues circular 97–00189 regarding the "combat against the reprehensible actions of sectarian movements," regarded as a "national priority." The Ministry called on groups such as UNADFI and CCMM to assist and for civil servants to investigate cultic groups with labor, health, and school inspections.

December 18, 1997: Official document of the American Embassy in Paris reveals religious and economic discrimination when the Church of Scientology International (in the United States) attempted to transfer funds to prevent the liquidation of French Scientology centers. Among other items, the document noted that the Investments of the French Ministry of Finance refused the transfer since the objective of the Minister of the Economy "was to put an end to the activities of the

Church of Scientology (Paris)." It also noted that the "French government opposed the activities of the Church of Scientology (Paris)" and that the church allegedly "constituted a threat to public order and security" (FOIA document number 95PARIS27046).

1998: Judge in a pending Scientology court case in Marseille (which dates to 1983) announces that court files are missing. This leads to rumors that Scientologists may have removed or destroyed them – a claim widely repeated in the media, nationally and internationally. Then-Minister of Justice Élisabeth Guigou accuses Scientologists of theft and asserts that the events raise the question of banning the Church of Scientology. However, the Public Prosecutor of Marseille soon after admits that the documents in question were accidentally destroyed by the court itself, along with three tons of other materials (representing 1,788 cases) unrelated to the Scientology case.

1998: Sociologist Régis Dericquebourg authors a study of French Scientologists, published in English as "Scientology: Its Cosmology, Anthropology, System of Ethics & Methodologies," in the Church of Scientology International's volume *Scientology: Theology & Practice of a Contemporary Religion.*

March 2, 1998: French National School for the Judiciary holds five days of sessions on cults at the request of the Minister of Justice. More than 100 judges participate, as well as anticult actors and associations. These training sessions for judges have since occurred annually. They include sessions on specific movements that are led by opponents of the groups in question.

March 23, 1998: A report from the French State's Observatory on Cults is rendered to the Prime Minister. Scientology is targeted and the report advises, *inter alia*, to allow anticult associations to be plaintiffs in criminal trials involving cults, even if they did not suffer damages.

May 1998: *Éducation civique, 4e: Libertés, droits, justice* (Civic Education #4: Freedoms, Rights, Justice) published. Scientology's Purification Rundown is falsely described as "one week of fasting with prescription of vitamins: 12000 FF."

June 16, 1998: The Administrative Court of Strasbourg cancels the decision of the Prefect to refuse the registration of a religious association belonging to the Church of Scientology, stating that "the administration does not provide any evidence that its activity is likely to threaten public order."

October 7, 1998: Governmental decree 98–890 creates an interministerial mission to fight against cults (MILS) to replace the Interministerial Observatory on Cults. The first President is Alain Vivien. Scientologists protest the decree as unconstitutional and a violation of laws concerning the separation of church and state.

October 30, 1998: The Malton case (from the name of a former Scientologist who was prompted by UNADFI to lodge a complaint) against the Church of Scientology Celebrity Centre of Paris and SEL/SARL (which sells Hubbard books) begins. More than fifty Scientologist staff and parishioners will be questioned by police, and the investigation will involve police raids of Celebrity Centre and SEL, with accounting documents seized. Five Scientologists will be indicted.

November 30, 1998: Following a report by UNADFI to the General Confederation of Labour (*Confédération Générale du Travail*, CGT) trade union at the Gravelines nuclear power plant, Pierre Denis, an engineer and Scientologist, was denied a promotion to operations manager. The groups UNADFI and CGT blame EDF (Electricity of France, a French State company) for allowing Denis to be employed in the first place. He is then transferred and sidelined to another position in Lyon. There is extensive and sensationalistic media coverage over the events. Due to discrimination and harassment, Denis later leaves France to live in the United States.

December 5, 1998: A young girl is refused registration with the Scouts organization in France because her mother and stepfather are Scientologists.

December 1998: French parliamentary commission on "cults and money" is set up (the second parliamentary commission on cults by this date).

April 24, 1999: The Parliamentary Commission of Inquiry requires sixty so-called *sectes* to submit a twenty-nine-page questionnaire on their finances, with questions about the names of all debtors and creditors, the names of all officers and members of the Board of Directors, a declaration of all relationships with other legal entities, a declaration of all assets, and so on. The Church of Scientology refuses, along with other religious groups. There is no penalty, though the refusal is technically illegal and could have been punished with prison time.

May 1999: Georges Fenech publishes *Face aux sectes: Politique, Justice, Etat* (Faced with Cults: Politics, Justice, State) with PUF (Presses universitaires de France).

June 1999: Commission of Inquiry into Sectes publishes report *Les sectes et l'argent* (Cults and Money).

June 15, 1999: Police raid Vincennes Institut Aubert, a private school directed by a Scientologist.

December 20, 1999: Ministry of the Interior releases circular "relating to the fight against the reprehensible acts of cultic movements" (99 0026 2C). It emphasizes "the place of the prefects in the system of fight against the reprehensible acts of cultic movements."

1999: Sociologists Françoise Champion and Martine Cohen publish *Sectes et Démocratie* (Cults and Democracy).

1999: *La Scientologie est-elle au-dessus des lois?* (Is Scientology Above the Law?), a French TV documentary (France 2 channel), is produced. It is broadcast the following year on Australia's SBS channel.

February 7, 2000: First annual report of MILS published. Two groups in particular are targeted: the Order of the Solar Temple and Church of Scientology.

2000: Paris Scientology center raided twice by CNIL (*Commission Nationale de l'Informatique et des Libertés*), an independent body in charge of ensuring respect of the law on data protection.

May 16, 2000: Police raid Paris Scientology center.

June 2000: Police raid Lyon Scientology center.

June 2000: Narconon Leman center is liquidated by the state after filing bankruptcy in light of tax liabilities totaling more than 2 million francs (an amount disputed as unlawful). During this time, the center was under criminal investigation, and later cleared of wrongdoing on January 24, 2005.

July 6, 2000: Defamation case filed by anti-Scientology activist Bob Minton. The church had sent a letter to the media regarding a visit to Paris by Minton (and Stacy Brooks). The case was ultimately resolved in favor of the Church of Scientology on appeal in 2002.

October 2, 2000: Workplace discrimination of Maryvonne Legoux, a librarian who was demoted due to her membership in the Church of Scientology. She challenged the decision and an administrative court of Levallois-Perret judged that the demotion was illegal. However, the city and library where she was employed failed to offer any compensation or remedy.

December 2000: Release of the second annual report of MILS, criticizing the latest report of the US State Department on Religious Freedom.

February 2001: Sociologist Danièle Hervieu-Léger publishes *La religion en miettes ou la question des sectes* (Religion in Shreds, or the Question of Cults) with Calmann-Lévy.

March 19, 2001: Police raid the Paris Scientology church and Paris Celebrity Centre, along with the homes of ten Scientologists.

April 2001: The French media begins to publish articles about Panda's antiviral software programs with false claims about its uses to infiltrate government databases. Panda is one of the international leaders in cybersecurity and its founder is a Scientologist. The negative publicity leads to loss of government contracts and sales for Panda.

May 2001: A two-year-old child in Paris is denied admission to a day nursery (*crèche*) because the parents are members of the Church of Scientology.

June 2001: About-Picard Law passed and introduces brainwashing theory into French courts. The legislation allows for the possible dissolution of groups based on their alleged psychological practices, inventing a new crime of "abuse of weakness through psychological subjection." Associations granted public utility status, such as UNADFI, are permitted under this law to participate in criminal proceedings against *sectes* and minority groups even if they were not victims themselves.

July 28, 2001: At the order of French authorities, Scientology vessel *Freewinds* is searched by the Antillean–Guyana ship security center in St. Barthélemy.

September 2001: University diploma program created in *victimologie liée à la nuisance sectaire* (victimology linked to cultic harm) at the Faculty of Medicine of Claude Bernard University Lyon 1. Lecturers in the program include Jean-Marie Abgrall, Jean-Michel Pesenti, and Jean-Pierre Jougla.

November 2001: MILS publishes an educator's guide on the "cultic phenomenon." Scientology is referred to as a *secte absolue* (absolute cult), the designation considered most dangerous to the public.

November 2001: Distribution in French public schools of a miniature book (as small as a thumb) on the danger of *sectes*.

November 5, 2001: Beginning of discriminatory acts against Martine Rhein, a public school teacher in the seventeenth arrondissement (district) of Paris, due to her membership in the Church of Scientology.

November 24, 2001: Protest organized by the anticult organization "Attention enfants" in opposition to the opening of a new Church of Scientology in the seventeenth arrondissement of Paris. Protestors, who include the mayor of the district, throw eggs and other objects at Scientologists. Police are called in to restore order.

2001: Sociologist Régis Dericquebourg publishes *Croire et guérir: Quatre religions de guérison* (Believe and Heal: Four Healing Religions) with Dervy.

February 2002: Third annual MILS report published, again classifying Scientology as a *secte absolue* (absolute cult).

April 14, 2002: *Restricted Zone*, an M6 television program presented by Bernard de La Villardière on Scientology, airs.

July 23, 2002: Press conference held by the Church of Scientology in Paris. Church spokeswoman Danièle Gounord releases information on spending habits and international travel expenses of MILS officials such as Alain Vivien.

July 29, 2002: Police raid Paris Scientology center and Celebrity Centre.

September 2002: Sociologist Bruno Étienne publishes *La France face aux sectes* (France Faced with Cults) with Hachette.

September 2002: Catherine Picard and Anne Fournier, a project manager at MILS, publish *Sectes, démocratie et mondialisation* (Cults, Democracy, and Globalization) with PUF.

November 7, 2002: Bomb threat at the Paris Org. A man entered the church around 1:30 PM and claimed that a device would explode, before disappearing. Staff and parishioners are evacuated. Police search the building and no bomb is found.

November 28, 2002: MILS disbanded, and MIVILUDES formed.

February 5, 2003: The Court of Appeal of Paris confirms the conviction of Janine Tavernier, the President of UNADFI, for defamation against Danièle Gounord, spokesperson of the Church of Scientology.

March 2003: Academic conference against *sectes* held at the IUFM (University Teacher Training Institute) in Limoges.

May 2003: Arnaud Palisson publishes *Grande enquête sur la scientologie: Une secte hors la loi* (Major Investigation into Scientology, an Outlaw Cult) with Favre, based on his law thesis.

July 30, 2003: The *Conseil d'État* (the highest jurisdiction for judging administrative matters) issues a judgment in favor of Michel Raoust, a Scientologist, in response to the *Renseignements Généraux* (Intelligence Service) blocking access to his secret police files with personal information. This decision sets a precedent for access to personal files held by intelligence services in France.

August 2003: Alain Vivien publishes *Sectes* (Cults) with Éditions Odile Jacob.

October 2003: MIVILUDES organizes a university seminar on "Cults and Secularism," with support from the Ministry of Research. The seminar is held every two weeks through June 2004 at the École Pratique des Hautes Études in Paris.

October 2003: The Church of Scientology of Paris and its president, Marc Walter, are acquitted of charges in a fraud case, but convicted for violation of data protection, after allowing the church to send a letter to someone who had asked to be removed from its files. They are fined 5,000 euros.

December 2003: Stasi Commission releases report and recommendations on secularism, including proposed legislation to ban wearing overtly religious symbols. President Jacques Chirac presents the report to the Parliament.

March 2004: French law passed banning the display of overt religious symbols in public schools.

September 2004: Tom Cruise meets with then-Finance Minister Nicolas Sarkozy in Paris.

December 2004: Mayor of Angers attempts to block the sale of Hubbard books in an outdoor marketplace. An administrative court in Nantes intervenes, allows the sale of books, and fines the mayor 1,200 euros, payable to *Scientologie Espace Librairie* (SARL).

2004: Church of Scientology in Paris moves to a new site (7 rue Jules Cesar) with three organizational expressions: *Association Spirituelle de l'Eglise de Scientologie* (which traces to 1995, under the 1901 association law), SARL, which sells Hubbard books, and a worship association (church), *Eglise de Scientologie d'Ile de France* (in line with France's 1905 associations law).

2004: CICNS (*Centre d'Information et de Conseil des Nouvelles Spiritualités*, Centre of Information and Consultation on New Spiritualities) in operation. Among other activities, the group holds a conference in Paris in September 2007 and in 2009 releases a documentary, *La France antisectes: état des lieux* (Anticult France: State of Play).

2005: Master's degree program in "Religions and Societies" begins at Université Bordeaux-Montaigne, headed by religious studies scholar and NRM historian Bernadette Rigal-Cellard.

May 2005: Prime Minister Jean-Pierre Raffarin declares that the Guyard Report should not be used to categorize groups as *sectes*. The head of MIVILUDES, Jean-Michel Roulet, states the Guyard list of 173 cults is "completely obsolete."

October 2005: Anti-Scientology demonstration held outside the Scientology headquarters on rue Jules Cesar in Paris. It is organized by Anne Hidalgo, then an elected member of the Council of Paris, who will become the Mayor of Paris in 2014.

October 2005: Scientologist Frédéric Grossman receives Freedom Medal from David Miscavige at the International Association of Scientologists anniversary meeting for his work against psychiatric abuses in France.

2006: Third French parliamentary commission on *sectes* convened.

March 24, 2006: The *Conseil d'État* (the highest jurisdiction for judging administrative matters) issues a judgment recognizing the nonprofit nature of Narconon.

October 2006: Scientologist Marc Arrighi receives Freedom Medal from David Miscavige at the International Association of Scientologists anniversary meeting for the humanitarian help he provided to victims of the 2004 tsunami in India.

December 2006: MIVILUDES publishes report "L'enfance volée: les mineurs victimes des sectes" ("Stolen Childhood: Minors Victimized by Cults") under the leadership of Georges Fenech, a vocal critic of Scientology as a judge and elected official.

June 2007: International CESNUR conference held in Bordeaux at the Université Michel de Montaigne.

December 15, 2008: Police raid both the Paris Celebrity Centre and Paris Org.

June 18, 2009: CAIMADES (*Cellule d'assistance et d'intervention en matière de dérives sectaires*; Assistance and Intervention Unit in Matters of Sectarian/Cultic Aberrations) raids both the Paris Scientology Org and Paris Celebrity Centre.

October 27, 2009: Church of Scientology in France convicted for "organized fraud" and ordered to pay 600,000 euros. Several Scientologists receive suspended prison sentences and are required to pay additional fines.

Decision will be confirmed in 2011 on appeal and upheld in 2013 by the Court of Cassation. Later, the Court of Cassation will find that the French State had mishandled the case and that the only remaining plaintiff, UNADFI, had committed an abuse of law by remaining a civil party in the trial (both the French State and UNADFI will be convicted for this).

2009: Georges Fenech, who became President of MIVILUDES, announces the group will not provide a public or official list of *sectes* in France and will instead make a "reference" list available upon request.

2009: FECRIS granted special consultative status by the United Nations.

October 2010: Scientologist and biochemist Robert Galibert receives Freedom Medal from David Miscavige at the International Association of Scientologists anniversary celebration for his work on drug prevention in France.

2011: Canadian sociologist and NRM scholar Susan J. Palmer publishes *The New Heretics of France* with Oxford University Press. The Church of Scientology is taken up as an example of the French government's "war on *sectes*."

2012: Éric Roux, then-spokesperson for the French Church of Scientology, publishes *Inquisition en bande organisée dans la France d'aujourd'hui* (Organized Gang, Inquisition in Today's France) with Les 3 Génies.

March 7, 2013: The Ministry of Finance sends a team to carry out an extensive tax inspection of the Celebrity Centre Paris, Paris Org, and Scientology's bookselling company. After two years of inspection, on February 6, 2015, the tax office closes the inspection after finding no wrongdoing.

October 2013: Court of Cassation upholds October 2009 fraud conviction against Scientology. In connection with these proceedings, UNADFI will later be convicted for "abuse of law" since it had no right to act in the trial (separately confirmed in 2015 by the French Court of Cassation). The French State will eventually also be convicted for miscarriage of justice after the Church of Scientology sued (also confirmed in 2015 by the French Court of Cassation).

January 24–25, 2014: International academic conference on Scientology held in Belgium (Antwerpen-Wilrijke), hosted by the Faculty for the Comparative Study of Religion and Humanism (FVG). Two of the organizers are French: Régis Dericquebourg and Bernadette Rigal-Cellard. The conference is held in Belgium, instead of France, due to public hostility.

Proceedings of the conference are published, in English and French, in *Acta Comparanda* (Subsidia IV).

April 8, 2014: The Administrative Court of Paris renders a judgment against the French National School for the Judiciary, which is instructed to release documents related to its annual training sessions on cults to the Church of Scientology. The French State is ordered to pay 1,000 euros in damages to the church for withholding documents.

November 20, 2015: UNADFI is convicted by the Court of Appeal of Paris for illegally participating in the Malton trial as a plaintiff. It is ordered to pay 21,000 euros in damages to the Church of Scientology and Scientologists. The decision will be confirmed by the Court of Cassation.

2016: American sociologist Stuart A. Wright and Canadian sociologist Susan J. Palmer publish *Storming Zion: Government Raids on Religious Communities* with Oxford University Press. The work examines, among topics, new religious groups in France, including raids on Scientology centers.

2017: Thierry Lamote publishes *L'envers obscène de la modernité: De la Scientologie à Daech* (The Obscene Reverse Side of Modernity: From Scientology to ISIS) with Hermann.

May 2017: Sociologist Régis Dericquebourg guest-edits special issue on Scientology for *Nova Religio: The Journal of Alternative and Emergent Religions*.

May 2018: *Bitter Winter: A Magazine on Religious Liberty and Human Rights* magazine launched by CESNUR. It is international in scope and focuses on China, but also includes articles about new religions and minority groups in France, among other topics.

2018: Éric Roux publishes *Tout savoir sur la scientologie* (Everything You Need to Know About Scientology) with Pierre-Guillaume de Roux.

December 18, 2018: The Court of Appeal of Caen convicts Georges Fenech, former president of MIVILUDES and a rabid opponent of Scientology, for violating a presumption of innocence concerning the Celebrity Centre of Paris.

2019: Bernadette Rigal-Cellard publishes an extensive article entitled "The Visible Expansion of Scientology and its Actors" in *The Journal of CESNUR*.

2019: Éric Roux publishes *L'improbable banquet: quand scientologues et francs-maçons se mettent à table* (The Improbable Banquet: When Scientologists and Freemasons Sit Down at the Table) with Le Nouvel Athanor.

February 2021: Jean-François Six, the Catholic priest depicted as an "éminence grise" of the anticult association CCMM during the 1980s and the 1990s, found guilty by an ecclesiastical tribunal in Rome of sexual abuse and later defrocked. This decision will be confirmed on appeal in 2022.

March 2021: Bernadette Rigal-Cellard publishes the article "Do Not Dare Speak of Scientology in France!" in *Implicit Religion: Journal for the Critical Study of Religion*.

December 21, 2021: The Administrative Court of Appeal of Paris issues a judgment convicting the French State and the city of Saint-Denis for misuse of power, after they deny a construction work request for the future Ideal Org of Greater Paris, based on opposition to the opening by some local authorities.

2022: Italian NRM scholar Massimo Introvigne and French religious studies scholar Bernadette Rigal-Cellard publish coedited volume *La Scientology sur la scène religieuse et sociale contemporaine* (Scientology on the Contemporary Religious and Social Scene) with EME Éditions.

2022: Politician Sonia Backès, a second-generation (former) Scientologist, takes up a position within the Macron government with MIVILUDES under her purview. Backès resigns the following year, after losing a senate race in New Caledonia, but during a brief tenure she called for reforms to monitor and regulate groups such as Scientology. This included opposition to the church's project to build an Ideal Organization in the Paris suburb of Saint-Denis.

2022: Éric Roux elected as Global Council Trustee for Europe at URI (United Religions Initiative, an international organization and the largest interfaith grassroots organization in the world). Roux is the first Scientologist to hold this position, and will later be appointed to URI's executive council.

January 9, 2024: Gabriel Attal appointed prime minister in the Macron government. The previous year, as education minister, Attal banned the wearing of abayas by Muslims in public schools.

April 6, 2024: Church of Scientology and Celebrity Centre of Greater Paris (Ideal Org) opened in the Paris suburb of Saint-Denis.

June 2024: International CESNUR conference held in Bordeaux for the second time.

July–August 2024: Summer Olympics in Paris. The Olympic stadium, in Saint-Denis, is within walking distance of the new Church of Scientology and Celebrity Centre of Greater Paris.

References

Abgrall, J. M. (2002). *Le mécanique des sectes*. Revised and expanded edition (originally published 1996). Paris: Payot.

Ables, K. (2023). U.N. Criticizes French Move to Bar Olympians from Wearing Headscarves. *The Washington Post*, September 28. www.washington post.com/world/2023/09/28/un-france-olympics-hijab-ban/.

Adeliyan Tous, S., Richardson, J. T., & Taghipour, A. (2023). Using Law to Limit Religious Freedom: The Case of New Religious Movements in France. *Religions, 14*(887), 1–23.

Adenor, J. L. (2022). Sonia Backès: "Nous devons travailler sur l'arsenal législatif autour de l'emprise mentale," November 2. www.marianne.net/societe/sante/sonia-backes-nous-devons-travailler-sur-larsenal-legislatif-autour-de-lemprise-mentale.

Åkerbäck, P. (2018a). The Politicization of Children in Minority Religions: The Swedish and European Contexts. In L. Frisk, S. Nilsson, & P. Åkerbäck, eds., *Children in Minority Religions: Growing up in Controversial Religious Groups*, 17–39. Sheffield: Equinox.

Åkerbäck, P. (2018b). Recently Reborn: To Return as a Child of Scientologist Parents. In L. Frisk, S. Nilsson, & P. Åkerbäck, eds., *Children in Minority Religions: Growing up in Controversial Religious Groups*, 97–121. Sheffield: Equinox.

Altglas, V. (2008). French Cult Controversy at the Turn of the New Millennium: Escalation, Dissensions and New Forms of Mobilisations across the Battlefield. In E. Barker, ed., *The Centrality of Religion in Social Life: Essays in Honour of James A. Beckford*, 55–68. Farnham: Ashgate.

Altglas, V. (2010). *Laïcité* Is What *Laïcité* Does: Rethinking the French Cult Controversy. *Current Sociology, 58*(3), 489–510.

Anthony, D., & Robbins, T. (2004). Pseudoscience versus Minority Religions: An Evaluation of the Brainwashing Theories of Jean-Marie Abgrall. In J. T. Richardson, ed., *Regulating Religion: Case Studies from around the Globe*, 127–49. New York: Kluwer Academic.

Ariès, P. (1998). *La Scientologie: laboratoire du futur?* Villeurbanne: Éditions Golias.

Ariès, P. (1999). *La Scientologie: une secte contre la république*. Villeurbanne: Éditions Golias.

Arjona, I. P. (2017). My Thoughts on the Scientology Religious Order–the Sea Organization on its 50th Anniversary. *World Religion News*, August 12.

www.worldreligionnews.com/featured-contributors/scientologist-news-fea
tured-contributors/thoughts-scientology-religious-order-sea-organization-
50th-anniversary/.

Arjona, I. P. (2021). Comentario a la sentencia del tribunal administrativo de
apelación del estado de Baviera, del 16 de junio de 2021, por la que se declara
incompatible con la libertad religiosa y el principio de igualdad, la exclusión
de una adjudicación de subvenciones públicas a los miembros de
Scientology. *Laicidad y libertades: Escritos jurídicos*, *12*, 43–70.

Arjona, I. P., & Carrión, G. (2020). *El poder de la Palabra: Una guía para
conocer la verdad sobre Scientology*. Brussels: Walking Away and FORB
Press.

Arweck, E. (2006). *Researching New Religious Movements: Responses and
Redefinitions*. London: Routledge.

Arweck, E., & Clarke, P. B. (1997). *New Religious Movements in Western
Europe: An Annotated Bibliography*. Westport, CT: Greenwood Press.

Backès, S. (2023). Sonia Backès: "Pour lutter contre les dérives sectaires,
l'action de l'Etat doit changer d'échelle." *Le Figaro*, March 8. www.lefi
garo.fr/vox/societe/sonia-backes-pour-lutter-contre-les-derives-sectaires-l-
action-de-l-etat-doit-changer-d-echelle-20230308.

Barker, E. (2024). Why the New French Law on "Cults" Is Wrong. *Bitter
Winter*, February 20. https://bitterwinter.org/why-the-new-french-law-on-
cults-is-wrong/.

Baubérot, J. (1999). Laïcité, Sectes, Société. In F. Champion, & M. Cohen, eds.,
Sectes et démocraties, 314–30. Paris: Seuil.

Baubérot, J. (2014). *Laïcité* and Freedom of Conscience in Pluricultural France.
In J. Berlinerblau, S. Fainberg, & A. Nou, eds., *Secularism on the Edge:
Rethinking Church-State Relations in the United States, France, and Israel*,
103–11. New York: Palgrave Macmillan.

Baubérot, J. (2021). *Histoire de la laïcité en France*. Paris: Presses Universitaires
de France.

Beckford, J. A. (1981). Cults, Controversy and Control: A Comparative Analysis
of the Problems Posed by New Religious Movements in the Federal Republic
of Germany and France. *Sociological Analysis*, *42*(3), 249–64.

Beckford, J. A. (2004). "Laïcité," "Dystopia," and the Reaction to New Religious
Movements in France. In J. T. Richardson, ed., *Regulating Religion: Case
Studies from around the Globe*, 27–40. New York: Kluwer Academic.

Berzano, L., Falikov, B., Fautré, W. et al. (2022a). Sympathy for the Devil: The
Anticult Federation FECRIS and Its Support for Russian and Chinese
Repression of Religion. *The Journal of CESNUR*, *6*(3) (May–June), 25–67.

Berzano, L., Falikov, B., Fautré, W. et al. (2022b). Anticult Ideology and FECRIS: Dangers for Religious Freedom. *The Journal of CESNUR*, *6*(3) (May–June), 3–24.

Besier, G. (2017). The Cooperation between Church and State in Germany. *Religion–Staat–Gesellschaft*, *18*(1–2), 55–66.

Besier, G., & Seiwert, H., eds. (2012). *Freedom of Religion or Belief: Anti-Sect Movements and State Neutrality (A Case Study: FECRIS)*. *Religion–Staat–Gesellschaft*. Münster: LIT Verlag.

BFMTV. (2022). Dérives sectaires: la secrétaire d'État Sonia Backès répond aux questions de BFMTV, November 2. YouTube. www.youtube.com/watch?v=9gPjSqO-YLg.

Blum, M. (2023). Issue Update: Religious Freedom Concerns in the European Union, July. *USCIRF*. www.uscirf.gov/sites/default/files/2023-07/2023%20Status%20of%20FoRB%20Issue%20Update_07.19.pdf.

Boichot, L. (2022). Sectes: le combat intime de la secrétaire d'État Sonia Backès, "sauvée" des dérives scientologie. *Le Figaro*. www.lefigaro.fr/politique/lutte-contre-les-sectes-le-combat-intime-de-sonia-backes-la-ministre-rechappee-de-la-scientologie-20220926.

Bowen, J. R. (2007). *Why the French Don't Like Headscarves: Islam, the State, and Public Space*. Princeton, NJ: Princeton University Press.

Bowen, J. R. (2010). *Can Islam Be French? Pluralism and Pragmatism in a Secularist State*. Princeton, NJ: Princeton University Press.

Bromley, D. G., ed. (1998). *The Politics of Religious Apostasy: The Role of Apostates in the Transformation of Religious Movements*. Westport, CT: Praeger.

Campos, É. (2001). Le droit pénal français et la questions des sectes: Quelques réflexions autour d'une controverse. In J. Duhaime, & G.-R. St-Arnaud, eds., *La peur des sectes*, 177–200. Montréal: Les Éditions Fides.

Carobene, G. (2017). Concerning the Research of a Juridical Identity for Scientology According to Recent European Case Law. *Acta Comparanda*, Subsidia IV, Proceedings of the International Conference: Scientology in a Scholarly Perspective (January 24–25, 2014), 21–32.

Chagnon, R. (1983). Nouvelles religions et quête d'identité: Le cas de l'Eglise de Scientologie de Montréal. *Studies in Religion/Sciences Religieuses*, *12*(4), 407–32.

Chagnon, R. (1985). *La Scientologie: Une Nouvelle Religion de la Puissance*. Ville de LaSalle, Québec: Hurtubise HMH.

Chagnon, R. (1987). Religion et santé: le cas de l'Eglise de Scientologie. *Social Compass*, *34*(4), 495–507.

Champion, F., & Cohen, M. (1999). *Sectes et démocratie*. Paris: Éditions du Seuil.

Chryssides, G. (2019). Key Data on Religions by Country. In G. Chryssides, ed., *Minority Religions in Europe and the Middle East*, 227–49. London: Routledge.

Churches of Scientology for Europe. (2022). The Druze and Scientology: A Conversation with Éric Roux and Sheikh Kasem Bader. YouTube. https://youtu.be/WMWZA_C6-hs.

Church of Scientology International. (2023a). David Miscavige: At the Helm in the Era of Expansion. www.scientology.org/david-miscavige/at-helm-in-era-of-expansion/.

Church of Scientology International. (2023b). The Scientology Religion in France. www.scientologyreligion.org/religious-recognitions/france.html.

Church of Scientology International. (2023c). France: Standing for Liberty in Paris. www.scientology.org/2023-celebrating-the-ias/#paris.

Church of Scientology International. (2024). "Personal Integrity" by L. Ron Hubbard. Originally published in *Ability*, Issue 125, February 1961. www.scientology.org/what-is-scientology/basic-principles-of-scientology/personal-integrity.html.

Claude, S. (2022). Une BD qui porte bien son nom avec la reparution de Dans la secte aux éditions La Boîte à Bulles le 5 janvier 2022. Publik Art. January 4. https://publikart.net/une-bd-qui-porte-bien-son-nom-avec-la-reparution-de-dans-la-secte-aux-editions-la-boite-a-bulles-le-5-janvier-2022/.

Council of Europe. (2020). European Convention on Human Rights. www.echr.coe.int/documents/d/echr/convention_ENG.

Courrier de l'Ouest. (1997). Un étudiant de 20 ans soupçonné d'avoir posé la bombe d'Angers, March 15. No author listed. Self-archived copy on Google Drive: https://drive.google.com/file/d/1N1xvriMg0_150KZem88ffxO3M8czMZhC/view?usp=sharing.

Cusack, C. M. (2020). Apostate Memoirs and the Study of Scientology in the Twenty-First Century. *Implicit Religion*, *23*(2), 148–55.

Darcondo, J. (1998). *La pieuvre scientologique*. Paris: Fayard.

Davis, S. M. (2020). *Rise of French Laïcité: French Secularism from the Reformation to the Twenty-First Century*. Eugene, OR: Pickwick.

Dericquebourg, R. (1998a). De la thérapie à la spiritualité et inversement: l'exemple de la scientologie et du rebirth. *Recherches sociologiques*, Université catholique de Louvain, *29*(2), 37–51.

Dericquebourg, R. (1998b). La controverse sur les sectes en France. *Fides*, Heritage et Projet. https://shs.hal.science/halshs-00087025.

Dericquebourg, R. (1998c). Scientology: Its Cosmology, Anthropology, System of Ethics & Methodologies. In *Scientology: Theology & Practice of a Contemporary Religion*, 163–75. Los Angeles: Bridge. Republished online

by the Church of Scientology International, www.scientologyreligion.org/
religious-expertises/scientology-cosmology-anthropology/.

Dericquebourg, R. (2000). Les stratégies des groupes religieux minoritaires face à la lutte antisecte française. *Religiologiques*, *22*, 119–30.

Dericquebourg, R. (2001). *Croire et guérir: Quatre religions de guérison*. Paris: Éditions Dervy.

Dericquebourg, R. (2011). Legitimizing Belief through the Authority of Science: The Case of the Church of Scientology. In J. R. Lewis & O. Hammer, eds., *Handbook of Religion and the Authority of Science*, 741–62. Leiden: Brill.

Dericquebourg, R. (2012). FECRIS: European Federation of Research and Information Centers on Sectarianism. *Religion–Staat–Gesellschaft*, *13*(2), 183–96.

Dericquebourg, R. (2017). The French Law of 1905 Founding "*Laïcité*" and Religious Freedom. *Religion–Staat–Gesellschaft*, *18*(1–2), 67–82.

Duval, P. (2018). State Neutrality and Anti-Sect Movements: The French Case. Law and Freedom of Belief in Europe Conference, 18-19 January 2018, Florence. Presentation available online, accessed November 14, 2023, https://vimeo.com/255263684.

Duval, P. (2021). More Money to MIVILUDES: The French "Mind Police" Is Back. *Bitter Winter*, April 19. https://bitterwinter.org/more-money-to-mivi ludes-the-french-mind-police-is-back/.

Duvert, C. (2004). Anticultism in the French Parliament: Desperate Last Stand or an Opportune Leap Forward? A Critical Analysis of the 12 June 2001 Act. In J. T. Richardson, ed., *Regulating Religion: Case Studies from around the Globe*, 41–52. New York: Kluwer Academic.

d'Eaubonne, F. (1982). *Dossier S . . . .comme sectes*. Paris: Éditions Alain Moreau.

Erhel, C., & de La Baume, R., eds. (1997). *Le Procès de l'Église de Scientologie: 30 Septembre – 8 Octobre 1996*. Paris: Albin Michel.

Fautré, W., Garay, A., & Nidegger, Y. (2004). The Sect Issue in the European Francophone Sphere. In T. Lindholm, W. C. Durham, B. G. Tahzib-Lie, E. A. Sewell, & L. Larsen, eds., *Facilitating Freedom of Religion or Belief: A Deskbook*, 595–618. Dordrecht: Springer Science+Business Media.

Fautré, W. (2023). France: FECRIS Tries Twice to Escape a Court Procedure – in Vain. *Bitter Winter*, December 19. https://bitterwinter.org/france-fecris-tries-twice-to-escape-a-court-procedure-in-vain/.

FECRIS. (2024). Homepage. www.fecris.org/.

Le Figaro. (2021). La justice confirme autoriser l'Église de scientologie à installer un centre à Saint-Denis, December 21. No author name given.

www.lefigaro.fr/actualite-france/la-justice-confirme-autoriser-l-eglise-de-scientologie-a-installer-un-centre-a-saint-denis-20211221.

Fisher, D. (2023). New Caledonia: Independence Leader Wins French Senate Seat over Macron Favourite. *The Interpreter*, October 3. Lowy Institute. www.lowyinstitute.org/the-interpreter/new-caledonia-independence-leader-wins-french-senate-seat-over-macron-favourite.

Fokas, E., & Richardson, J. T., eds. (2019). *The European Court of Human Rights and Minority Religions: Messages Generated and Messages Received*. London: Routledge.

Folk, H. (2019). The Church of Scientology in Hungary: A "Religious Multinationals" Case Study. In G. Chryssides, ed., *Minority Religions in Europe and the Middle East*, 162–76. London: Routledge.

Fouchereau, B. (1996). *La mafia des sectes: Du rapport de l'Assemblée nationale aux implications des multinationales*. Levallois-Perret: Filipacchi.

France 2. (2023). Victimes de sectes: de l'emprise à la reconstruction, March 28. www.france.tv/france-3/debat/4713922-victimes-de-sectes-de-l-emprise-a-la-reconstruction.html.

France Info. (2022). Interview with Sonia Backès, 8.30 FranceInfo. Reposted to YouTube. www.youtube.com/watch?v=4cWVQrBY1eU.

French National Assembly. (2019). Constitution of October 4, 1958. English translation. www2.assemblee-nationale.fr/langues/welcome-to-the-english-website-of-the-french-national-assembly#Title1.

French Republic. (2023). LOI no. 2023-22 du 24 janvier 2023 d'orientation et de programmation du ministère de l'intérieur (1). www.legifrance.gouv.fr/jorf/id/JORFTEXT000047046768.

Frisk, L. (2018). Applied Scholastics and Study Technology: The Educational Perspective Developed by L. Ron Hubbard. In L. Frisk, S. Nilsson, & P. Åkerbäck, eds., *Children in Minority Religions: Growing up in Controversial Religious Groups*, 382–97. Sheffield: Equinox.

Frisk, L., Nilsson, S., & Åkerbäck, P., eds. (2018). *Children in Minority Religions: Growing up in Controversial Religious Groups*. Sheffield: Equinox.

Garay, A. (2019). New Religious Movements in France: The Legal Situation. In G. D. Chryssides, ed., *Minority Religions in Europe and the Middle East*, 99–113. London: Routledge.

Guillon, P., & Alloing, L. (2021). *Dans la secte*. Saint-Avertin: La Boîte à Bulles.

Haarscher, G. (2021). *La laïcité*. Paris: Presses Universitaires de France.

Haskell, J. (2022). Karen Bass says it's "ridiculous" for Rick Caruso to associate her with the Church of Scientology. ABC7 Eyewitness News, Los Angeles, September 28. https://abc7.com/la-mayors-race-2022-karen-bass-rick-caruso-los-angeles-elections/12269452/.

Hervieu-Léger, D. (2001a). France's Obsession with the "Sectarian Threat." *Nova Religio, 4*(2), 249–57.

Hervieu-Léger, D. (2001b). *La Religion en miettes ou la question des sectes.* Paris: Calmann-Lévy.

Hervieu-Léger, D. (2004). France's Obsession with the "Sectarian Threat." In P. C. Lucas & T. Robbins, eds., *New Religious Movements in the Twenty-First Century: Legal, Political, and Social Challenges in Global Perspective,* 40–48. New York: Routledge.

Hubbard, L. R. (1951). *Science of Survival.* Wichita, KS: Hubbard Dianetic Foundation.

Hubbard, L. R. (1970). The Ideal Org. Executive Directive 102 International, May 20.

Hubbard, L. R. (1972). How to Handle Black Propaganda. Hubbard Communications Office Policy. PR Series 18, November 21.

Hubbard, L. R. (2007). *Dianetics: The Modern Science of Mental Health.* Los Angeles: Bridge. Originally published in 1950 by Hermitage House, New York.

IFOP. (2018). *Le regard des Français sur l'Eglise de Scientologie.* Paris. Copy provided to the author.

Internet Archive. (1990). We Stand Tall – Scientology Singers. Archived September 9, 2018. https://archive.org/details/WeStandTall.

Introvigne, M. (1995). The Secular Anticult and the Religious Counter-Cult Movement: Strange Bedfellows or Future Enemies? In R. Towler, ed., *New Religions and the New Europe,* 32–54. Aarhus: Aarhus University Press.

Introvigne, M. (1999). Defectors, Ordinary Leave-Takers, and Apostates: A Quantitative Study of Former Members of New Acropolis in France. *Nova Religio, 3*(1), 83–99.

Introvigne, M. (2000). Moral Panics and Anticult Terrorism in Western Europe. *Terrorism and Political Violence, 12*(1), 47–59.

Introvigne, M. (2004). Holy Mountains and Anticult Ecology: The Campaign against the Aumist Religion in France. In J. T. Richardson, ed., *Regulating Religion: Case Studies from around the Globe,* 73–83. New York: Kluwer Academic.

Introvigne, M. (2014). Scientology in Italy: Plagio and the Twenty Year Legal Saga. In J. T. Richardson, & Bellanger, eds., *Legal Cases, New Religious Movements, and Minority Faiths,* 25–36. Surrey: Ashgate.

Introvigne, M. (2017). Religious Freedom Problems in Russia and Hungary: A Case Study of the Church of Scientology. *Religion–Staat–Gesellschaft, 18* (1–2), 241–50.

Introvigne, M. (2018). Introduction: Scientology and the New Cult Wars. *The Journal of CESNUR*, *2*(2) (March–April), 4–10. https://doi.org/10.26338/tjoc.2018.2.2.1.

Introvigne, M. (2021). France's Strange War against the Jehovah's Witnesses. *Bitter Winter*, May 18. https://bitterwinter.org/frances-strange-war-against-the-jehovahs-witnesses/.

Introvigne, M. (2022a). *Brainwashing: Reality or Myth?* New York: Cambridge University Press.

Introvigne, M. (2022b). France: Is State Secretary Sonia Backès a "Scientology Survivor"? Her Brother Tells a Different Story. *Bitter Winter*, November 28. https://bitterwinter.org/is-france-state-secretary-sonia-backes-a-scientology-survivor/.

Introvigne, M. (2023a). France Joins China and Russia by Introducing Special Police Techniques against "Cults." *Bitter Winter*, February 1. https://bitter winter.org/france-special-police-techniques-against-cult.

Introvigne, M. (2023b). Anticultism à la Mode de Caen: To Avoid a Court Hearing, MIVILUDES Humors Scientology. *Bitter Winter*, May 5. https://bitterwinter.org/to-avoid-a-court-hearing-miviludes-humors-scientology/.

Introvigne, M. (2023c). MIVILUDES, from Tragedy to Farce: Bailiff Compels Georges Fenech to Pay His Debts to Scientology. *Bitter Winter*, May 19. https://bitterwinter.org/miviludes-bailiff-compels-georges-fenech-to-pay-his-debts-to-scientology/.

Introvigne, M. (2023d). An American Scholar Looks at Scientology in France–and at the Sonia Backès Saga. *Bitter Winter*, August 28. https://bitter winter.org/an-american-scholar-looks-at-scientology-in-france-and-at-the-sonia-backes-saga/.

Introvigne, M. (2023e). The Myth of a Russia Besieged by "Cults": From Ivan Ilyin to the Russian FECRIS' Campaigns against Scientology. *The Journal of CESNUR*, *7*(6) (November–December), 19–33. https://doi.org/10.26338/tjoc.2023.7.6.2.

Introvigne, M. (2023f). USCIRF Warns against New French Anticult Draft Law. *Bitter Winter*, December 13. https://bitterwinter.org/uscirf-warns-against-new-french-anti-cult-draft-law.

Introvigne, M., Amicarelli, A., Fautré, W., Rigal-Cellard, B., & Pansier, F. J. (2020). "Separatism," Religion, and "Cults": Religious Liberty Issues. November. White paper. CESNUR, Human Rights without Frontiers, and European Federation for Freedom of Belief.

Introvigne, M., & Melton, J. G., eds. (1996). *Pour en finir avec les sectes: Le débat sur le rapport de la commission parlementaire*. Paris: Éditions Dervy.

Introvigne, M., & Rigal-Cellard, B., eds. (2022). *La Scientology sur la scène religieuse et sociale contemporaine*. Louvain-la-Neuve: EME Éditions.

Kaiser, H. (1994). The American Connection of Certain Religious Bodies in the Paris Area. *Revue française d'études américaines*, *59*, 75–84.

Kent, S. A. (2001). The French and German versus American Debate over "New Religions," Scientology, and Human Rights. *Marburg Journal of Religion*, *6*(1), 1–63.

Koussens, D. (2023). *Secularism(s) in Contemporary France: Law, Policy, and Religious Diversity*. Translated by P. Feldstein. Cham, Switzerland: Springer Nature.

Kuru, A. T. (2009). *Secularism and State Policies toward Religion: The United States, France, and Turkey*. New York: Cambridge University Press.

Lenzini, J. (1996). *Scientologie: vol au-dessus d'un nid de gourous*. Toulon: Plein Sud.

Luca, N. (2004). Is There a Unique French Policy of Cults?: A European Perspective. In J. T. Richardson, ed., *Regulating Religion*, 53–72. New York: Kluwer Academic.

Luca, N., & Lenoir, F. (1998). *Sectes: Mensonges et idéaux*. Paris: Bayard Éditions.

Machi, H. (2013). The French System against Sectarian Deviations. In D. M. Kirkham, ed., *State Responses to Minority Religions*, 115–19. Surrey: Ashgate.

Máté-Tóth, A., & Nagy, G. D. (2011). *Alternatív vallás: Szcientológia Magyarországon*. Budapest: L'Harmattan.

Máté-Tóth, A., & Nagy, G. D. (2017). Not an Extraordinary Group: Scientologists in Hungary and Germany – Comparative Survey Data. In J. R. Lewis, & K. Hellesøy, eds., *Handbook of Scientology*, 141–56. Leiden: Brill.

Mayer, J. F. (2006). A Brief Overview of the Attitudes of Western European States towards New Religious Movements. Religioscope. *Research and Analyses*, *38* (November). http://religion.info/pdf/2016_11_nrms.pdf.

Melton, J. G., & Ashcraft, W. M. (2021). Ex-Member Accounts from New Religious Movements: A Compilation, 2000–Present. *The Journal of CESNUR*, *5*(6), 70–103. https://cesnur.net/wp-content/uploads/2021/11/tjoc_5_6_5_meltonashcraft.pdf.

Menu, Q. (2023). Battue aux sénatoriales, la secrétaire d'État à la Citoyenneté Sonia Backès démissionne du gouvernement. *France Info*. https://la1ere.francetvinfo.fr/battue-aux-senatoriales-la-secretaire-d-etat-a-la-citoyennete-sonia-backes-demissionne-du-gouvernement-1415012.html.

Miklovicz, A. (2021). Scientology and Physical Violence. *Sacra Journal*, *19*(2), 52–64. http://hdl.handle.net/11222.digilib/144743.

Miklovicz, A. (2023). From Mental Health to Spiritual Technology: The Evolution of Religious Practice in Scientology. *The Journal of CESNUR*, *7*(6) (November–December), 45–60.

MIVILUDES. (2022). 2021 Annual Report (revised, with response from Church of Scientology of France). www.miviludes.interieur.gouv.fr/sites/ default/files/publications/francais/MIVILUDES-RAPPORT2021_web_ %2027_04_2023%20_0.pdf.

MIVILUDES. (2023a). Qu'est-ce qu'une dérive sectaire?, www.miviludes .interieur.gouv.fr/quest-ce-quune-dérive-sectaire

MIVILUDES. (2023b). Santé, https://www.miviludes.interieur.gouv.fr/quest-ce-quune-d%C3%A9rive-sectaire/o%C3%B9-la-d%C3%A9celer/sant %C3%A9.

Le Monde. (1980). L'ancien président de l'Église de Scientologie relaxé, March 3. No author listed. www.lemonde.fr/archives/article/1980/03/03/l-ancien-president-de-l-eglise-de-scientologie-relaxe_2814780_1819218. html?xtmc=scientologie&xtcr=588.

Le Monde. (1981). La Scientologie est une "nouvelle discipline religieuse," February 23. No author listed. www.lemonde.fr//archives/article/1981/02/ 23/la-scientologie-est-une-nouvelle-discipline-religieuse_2706658_ 1819218.html.

Le Monde. (1984). Un Attentat Contre L'église De Scientologie Fait Un Blesse, April 4. No author listed. www.lemonde.fr/archives/article/1984/04/04/un-attentat-contre-l-eglise-de-scientologie-fait-un-blesse_3013578_1819218. html.

Le Monde. (1997). Les précédentes décisions de justice, July 30. No author listed (informational sidebar to articles by Jean-Michel Dumay and Cécile Prieur on Scientology and court cases), p. 7, July 30. Digital copy of newspaper available from Virginia Tech Library, https://scholar.lib.vt.edu/ InterNews/LeMonde/issues/1997/lm970730.pdf.

Morin, J. P. (1982). *Sectarus: Le violeur de conscience*. Nangis: Eboli.

Morton, J. (2020). The Anticult Movement and Religious Regulation in Russia and the Former Soviet Union. United States Commission on International Religious Freedom (USCIRF), Issue Update, July. www.uscirf.gov/sites/ default/files/2020%20Anticult%20Update%20-%20Religious%20 Regulation%20in%20Russia.pdf.

Négroni, A. (2023). Sonia Backès: "Il faut redonner une impulsion à notre politique pour lutter contre les dérives sectaires." *Le Figaro*, January 29. www.lefigaro.fr/actualite-france/sonia-backes-il-faut-redonner-une-impul sion-a-notre-politique-pour-lutter-contre-les-sectes-20230129.

Nilsson, S. (2017). New Religious Movements, Totalitarian Regimes, and Authoritarian Governments. *Religion–Staat–Gesellschaft*, *18*(1–2), 147–58.

Nilsson, S. (2024). *Children in New Religious Movements*. Cambridge: Cambridge University Press.

Ollion, É. (2013). The French "War on Cults" Revisited: Three Remarks on an Ongoing Controversy. In D. M. Kirkham, ed., *State Responses to Minority Religions*, 121–35. Surrey: Ashgate.

Palmer, S. J. (2002). France's Anti-Sect Wars. *Nova Religio*, *6*(1), 174–82.

Palmer, S. J. (2008). France's "War on Sects": A Post-9/11 Update. *Nova Religio*, *11*(3), 104–20.

Palmer, S. J. (2009). The Church of Scientology in France: Legal and Activist Counterattacks in the "War on Sects." In J. R. Lewis, ed., *Scientology*, 295–322. New York: Oxford University Press.

Palmer, S. J. (2011). *The New Heretics of France: Minority Religions*, la République, *and the Government-Sponsored "War on Sects."* New York: Oxford University Press.

Pansier, F. J. (2018). La Scientologie est-elle une religion? *The Journal of CESNUR*, Supplement to Vol. *2*(2) (March–April), I–LVII.

Pansier, F. J. (2022). La Scientology comme religion. In M. Introvigne & B. Rigal-Cellard, eds., *La Scientology sur la scène religieuse et sociale contemporaine*, 191–248. Louvain-la-Neuve: EME Éditions.

Pasquini, X. (1993). *Les sectes: Un mal profond de civilisation*. Paris: Jacques Grancher.

Petit-Castelli, C. (1979). *Les Sectes*. Paris: Éditions de Messine.

Ranc, P. (1993). *Une secte dangereuse: La Scientologie*. Saint-Légier: Editions Contrastes.

Reuters. (2023). No restrictions on hijab in Paris 2024 "Games" athletes village-IOC, September 29. www.reuters.com/sports/no-restrictions-hijab-paris-2024-games-athletes-village-ioc-2023-09-29/.

Richardson, J. T. (2009). Scientology in Court: A Look at Some Major Cases. In J. R. Lewis, ed., *Scientology*, 283–94. New York: Oxford University Press.

Richardson, J. T., ed. (2004). *Regulating Religion: Case Studies from around the Globe*. New York: Kluwer Academic.

Richardson, J. T., & Shoemaker, J. (2008). The European Court of Human Rights, Minority Religions, and the Social Construction of Religious Freedom. In E. Barker, ed., *The Centrality of Religion in Social Life: Essays in Honour of James A. Beckford*, 103–16. Farnham: Ashgate.

Richardson, J. T., & Bellanger, F., eds. (2014). *Legal Cases, New Religious Movements, and Minority Faiths*. Surrey: Ashgate.

Richardson, J. T., & Introvigne, M. (2001). "Brainwashing" Theories in European Parliamentary and Administrative Reports on "Cults" and "Sects." *Journal for the Scientific Study of Religion, 40*(2), 143–68.

Rigal-Cellard, B. (2019). The Visible Expansion of the Church of Scientology and Its Actors. *The Journal of CESNUR, 3*(1), 8–118.

Rigal-Cellard, B. (2021). "Do Not Dare Speak of Scientology in France!" *Implicit Religion, 23*(2), 182–92.

Rothstein, M. (2014). Emblematic Architecture and the Routinization of Charisma in Scientology. *International Journal for the Study of New Religions, 5*(1), 51–76.

Roux, É. (2012). *France 2012: Inquisition En Bande Organisée*. Paris: Génies.

Roux, É. (2014). Recent Developments in Relation to the RELIGARE Project Report. In M. C. Foblets, K. Alidadi, J. S. Nielsen, & Z. Yanasmayan, eds., *Belief, Law and Politics: What Future for a Secular Europe?* 275–82. New York: Routledge (2016). First published by Ashgate, 2014.

Roux, É. (2017). Postscript. *Acta Comparanda*, Subsidia IV, Proceedings of the International Conference: Scientology in a Scholarly Perspective (January 24–25, 2014), 263–72.

Roux, É. (2018). *Tout Savoir Sur La Scientologie*. Paris: Pierre-Guillaume de Roux.

Roux, É. (2019). *L'improbable banquet: quand scientologues et francs-maçons se mettent à table*. Paris: Le Nouvel Athanor.

Roux, É. (2021a). Scientology behind the Scenes: The Law Changer. In E. Barker & J. T. Richardson, eds., *Reactions to the Law by Minority Religions*, 58–78. New York: Routledge.

Roux, É. (2021b). Academic Study of Scientology: The Scientology Perspective. *Implicit Religion, 23*(2), 175–81.

Roux, É. (2023a). Qui sont 'les sectes'? *Rebelle[s]*, December 16. https://rebelles-lemag.com/2023/12/16/qui-sont-les-sectes/.

Roux, É. (2023b). Qui sont les sectes? Partie 2. *Rebelle[s]*, December 19. https://rebelles-lemag.com/2023/12/19/qui-sont-les-sectes-partie-2/.

Roux, É. (2023c). Qui sont les sectes ? Partie 3 et fin. *Rebelle[s]*, December 21. https://rebelles-lemag.com/2023/12/21/qui-sont-les-sectes-partie-3-et-fin/.

Siuberski, P. (2016). Belgian Court Rejects Case against Scientology, March 11. *Yahoo*. www.yahoo.com/lifestyle/belgian-court-throws-case-against-scientology-branch-002415553.html.

Smith, H. C. (2000). *Liberté, Egalité, et Fraternité* at Risk for New Religious Movements in France. *BYU Law Review, 26*(3), 1099–152.

Šorytė, R. (2021a). Labeling Scientology: "Cult," "Fringe," "Extremist," or Mainstream? *The Journal of CESNUR, 5*(4) (July–August), 58–76.

Šorytė, R. (2021b). Scientology, Anticultists, and Scholars: An Interview with Bernadette Rigal-Cellard. *Bitter Winter*, April 14. https://bitterwinter.org/scientology-anticultists-and-scholars-an-interview-with-bernadette-rigal-cellard/.

Šorytė, R. (2022). Scientology, Jehovah's Witnesses, "Cults," and Conspiracy Theories in Russia before and during the War in Ukraine. *The Journal of CESNUR, 6*(6) (November–December), 47–73.

Šorytė, R. (2023). Russian Anti-Scientology Technology and the Ukrainian War. *The Journal of CESNUR, 7*(6) (November–December), 3–18. https://doi.org/10.26338/tjoc.2023.7.6.1.

Ternisien, X. (2001). France: A Separate Crime of "Mental Manipulation" Disappears from the Draft Anticult Law, but the Substance of the Law Remains Unaltered. CESNUR. https://web.archive.org/web/20220524000329/https://www.cesnur.org/2001/jan12.htm.

Tervé, C. (2022). Sonia Backès raconte son enfance auprès de sa mère scientologue, *HuffPost.* www.huffingtonpost.fr/politique/article/sonia-backes-raconte-son-enfance-aupres-de-sa-mere-scientologue_209780.html.

United Religions Initiative (URI) (2023). Éric Roux. Global Council Trustee for Europe. https://web.archive.org/web/20231207140924/www.uri.org/eric-roux.

Urban, H. B. (2011). *The Church of Scientology: A History of a New Religion.* Princeton, NJ: Princeton University Press.

US Department of State. (2021). 2021 Report on International Religious Freedom: France. www.state.gov/reports/2021-report-on-international-religious-freedom/france/.

Van Eck Duymaer van Twist, A. (2015). *Perfect Children: Growing Up on the Religious Fringe.* New York: Oxford University Press.

Weightman, M. (2020). Scientology and Times of Uncertainty. In M. Francis & K. Knott, eds., *Minority Religions and Uncertainty*, 149–70. London: Routledge.

Westbrook, D. A. (2014). Freedom of Religion as a Human Right: The Council of Europe's Upcoming Vote on Establishing "Sect Observatories." *World Religion News*, March 19. www.worldreligionnews.com/religion-news/freedom-religion-human-right-council-europes-upcoming-vote-establishing-sect-observatories/.

Westbrook, D. A. (2018). The Art of PR War: Scientology, the Media, and Legitimation Strategies for the 21st Century. *Studies in Religion/Sciences Religieuses, 47*(3), 373–95.

Westbrook, D. A. (2019). *Among the Scientologists: History, Theology, and Praxis*. New York: Oxford University Press.

Westbrook, D. A. (2022). *L. Ron Hubbard and Scientology Studies*. New York: Cambridge University Press.

Westbrook, D. A. (2023). The War Is Not Over: Scientology, Resilience, and the Resurgence of State-Sponsored Anticultism in France. *International Journal for the Study of New Religions*, *12*(1), 115–43.

Willaime, J. P. (2010). The Paradoxes of *Laïcité* in France. In E. Barker, ed., *The Centrality of Religion in Social Life: Essays in Honour of James A. Beckford*, 41–54. Translated by A. Hardyck. Farnham: Ashgate.

WISE. (2022). What Is L. Ron Hubbard's Administrative Technology? World Institute of Scientology Enterprises. https://wise.org/what-is-l-ron-hubbards-administrative-technology/.

Woodrow, A. (1977). *Les nouvelles sectes*. Paris: Éditions du Seuil.

Wright, S. A., & Palmer, S. J. (2016). *Storming Zion: Government Raids on Religious Communities*. New York: Oxford University Press.

Wright, S. A., & Palmer, S. J. (2018). Countermovement Mobilization and State Raids on Minority Religious Communities. *Journal for the Scientific Study of Religion*, *57*(3), 616–33.

Acknowledgments

I am grateful to the numerous scholars, human rights leaders, and legal experts who corresponded with me in preparation for this work. Éric Roux, Vice President of the Church of Scientology's European Office for Public Affairs and Human Rights (Brussels), coordinated my interviews and fieldwork in Paris and Brussels (January and September 2023) and was indispensable, patiently answering questions and helping however he could. Interview material from my first trip (January 2023) was published in an article, "The War is Not Over: Scientology, Resilience, and the Resurgence of State-Sponsored Anticultism in France," *International Journal for the Study of New Religions* (2023), portions of which served as the starting point for this Element, especially material in Sections 1 and 2. Éric and I first met in 2014 at an international conference on Scientology hosted by the FVG in Antwerp. In the intervening years, he has been most helpful, bringing a French and broader European perspective informed by numerous "hats" – Scientologist, author, religious freedom and human rights advocate, interfaith activist, and lawyer. Edward E. Marsh, a longtime American Scientologist and collector, should also be noted. Marsh's private library in Rosarito, Mexico yielded unexpected but rich material relevant to Dianetics and Scientology in France, including correspondence between L. Ron Hubbard and John M. "Jack" Campbell, an early and important figure in Paris. Thanks are also due to Jean LeFebvre and Cathy Norman (Church of Scientology of Austin, Texas) for allowing me to view recordings of the 2023 International Association of Scientologists (IAS) anniversary celebrations. My son, Noah Westbrook, helped organize transcripts of Hubbard lectures from the 1950s and early 1960s as I searched for references to France and French Scientology. Finally, I am deeply thankful to Rebecca Moore, the NRM Element series editor for Cambridge University Press, for supporting this project, and to the many scholars who paved the path with their research on France and *sectes*, in both French and English publications: Bernadette Rigal-Cellard, Massimo Introvigne, Susan J. Palmer, Stuart A. Wright, James T. Richardson, Régis Dericquebourg, and Frédéric-Jérôme Pansier, to name but a few whose work made mine possible.

Cambridge Elements ⁼

New Religious Movements

Founding Editor

†James R. Lewis
Wuhan University

The late James R. Lewis was a Professor of Philosophy at Wuhan University, China. He was the author or co-author of 128 articles and reference book entries, and editor or co-editor of 50 books. He was also the general editor for the *Alternative Spirituality and Religion Review* and served as the associate editor for the *Journal of Religion and Violence*. His prolific publications include *The Cambridge Companion to Religion and Terrorism* (Cambridge University Press 2017) and *Falun Gong: Spiritual Warfare and Martyrdom* (Cambridge University Press 2018).

Series Editor

Rebecca Moore
San Diego State University

Rebecca Moore is Emerita Professor of Religious Studies at San Diego State University. She has written and edited numerous books and articles on Peoples Temple and the Jonestown tragedy. Publications include *Beyond Brainwashing: Perspectives on Cultic Violence* (Cambridge University Press 2018) and *Peoples Temple and Jonestown in the Twenty-First Century* (Cambridge University Press 2022). She is reviews editor for *Nova Religio*, the quarterly journal on new and emergent religions published by the University of Pennsylvania Press.

About the Series

Elements in New Religious Movements go beyond cult stereotypes and popular prejudices to present new religions and their adherents in a scholarly and engaging manner. Case studies of individual groups, such as Transcendental Meditation and Scientology, provide in-depth consideration of some of the most well known, and controversial, groups. Thematic examinations of women, children, science, technology, and other topics focus on specific issues unique to these groups. Historical analyses locate new religions in specific religious, social, political, and cultural contexts. These examinations demonstrate why some groups exist in tension with the wider society and why others live peaceably in the mainstream. The series highlights the differences, as well as the similarities, within this great variety of religious expressions. To discuss contributing to this series please contact Professor Moore.

Cambridge Elements $\overline{\overline{}}$

New Religious Movements

Elements in the Series

A full series listing is available at: www.cambridge.org/ENRM

Printed in the United States
by Baker & Taylor Publisher Services